"In the plethora of textbooks on IR almost none depart from 'playing it safe', giving forms of instruction in the rudiments of established theories. The great breakout of this volume is its entire second half of proposing quite radical new ways of looking at the world. The book is both 'safe' and 'unsafe' and in both it is sometimes witty in a way that students will savour – learning what IR is, and what it could be. A lovely book in which even the doyens of 'old' IR are sometimes bold."

– Stephen Chan OBE, Professor of World Politics, School of Oriental & African Studies, University of London.

"This rich volume offers a highly accessible and exceptionally broad-ranging introduction to the field of International Relations theory. In 20 short chapters the book provides a highly readable and comprehensive overview of core theoretical frameworks ranging from 'mainstream' realism and liberalism all the way to queer theory and critical geography. By placing each theory in context, and by providing a wealth of easily graspable examples, the book provides 'one-stop shopping' for the full range of theoretical frameworks and concepts – along with welcome attention to non-western perspectives. An excellent place to start."

– Mette Eilstrup-Sangiovanni, Senior University Lecturer in International Relations at Cambridge University.

"This is a superb book. It offers a comprehensive listing that is imaginatively presented and enormously accessible. Helpfully, too, it takes the form of a global conversation. IR theory at its sparkling best."

– Peter Vale, Professor of Humanities, University of Johannesburg; Professor of Public Policy and Global Affairs, Nanyang Technological University and Nelson Mandela Professor of Politics Emeritus, Rhodes University.

International Relations Theory

EDITED BY

STEPHEN MCGLINCHEY, ROSIE WALTERS
& CHRISTIAN SCHEINPFLUG

E-INTERNATIONAL RELATIONS PUBLISHING

E-International Relations
www.E-IR.info
Bristol, England
2017

ISBN 978-1-910814-19-2 (paperback)
ISBN 978-1-910814-20-8 (e-book)

Production: Michael Tang
Copy-editing: Gill Gairdner
Cover Image: feedough via Depositphotos

A catalogue record for this book is available from the British Library.

E-IR Foundations

Series Editor: Stephen McGlinchey
Editorial Assistants: Michael Bolt, Eloise Cox, Gary Leigh and Farah Saleem.

E-IR Foundations is a series of beginner's textbooks from E-International Relations (E-IR) that are designed to introduce complicated issues in a practical and accessible way. Each book will cover a different area connected to International Relations. This is the second book in the series, with more to follow.

You can find the books, and many other learning materials, on E-IR's Student Portal: http://www.e-ir.info/students

E-IR is developing our Foundations series as part of our mission to provide the best source of freely available scholarly materials for students of International Relations. Each book is available to buy in bookstores in paperback and, uniquely for textbooks, also freely accessible in web and PDF formats. So, readers can have each book at their fingertips and on all their devices without any restrictions or hassle.

Typically, textbook publishing is designed to appeal to professors/lecturers and, consequently, even the introductory books are intended less as an aid to the student and more to assist the instructor in the classroom. Our books are designed to meet the needs of the student, with the focus on moving readers from no prior knowledge to competency. They are intended to accompany, rather than replace, other texts, while offering the student a fresh perspective.

About E-International Relations

E-International Relations is the world's leading open access website for students and scholars of international politics, reaching over three million readers per year. E-IR's daily publications feature expert articles, blogs, reviews and interviews – as well as student learning resources. The website is run by a non-profit organisation based in Bristol, UK and staffed by an all-volunteer team of students and scholars.

http://www.e-ir.info

Acknowledgements

This book would not have been possible without the assistance of E-IR's Student Review Panel. Members of the panel gave up their spare time to read drafts of each chapter and offer their thoughts on how they could be improved. The panel comprised Laura Southgate, Matthew Koo, Constance Dijkstra, Loveleena Sharma, Daniel Golebiewski, Ljupcho Stojkovski, Max Nurnus, Jess Dam, Caroline Cottet, Jan Tattenberg, Matthew Ribar, Laura Cartner, Cameran Clayton, Phoebe Gardner, Ana Carolina Sarmento, Naomi McMillen, Kanica Rakhra, Dean Cooper-Cunningham, Jonathan Webb, Daniel Rowney, Janja R. Avgustin and Scott Edwards.

The editors would also like to thank all members of the E-International Relations team, past and present, for their many acts of kindness in feeding back on ideas and providing a supportive climate for the book's development.

Finally, and most importantly, the editors would like to thank the authors of each of the chapters for working so hard on this project and helping us deliver such an excellent book.

Contents

GETTING STARTED WITH INTERNATIONAL RELATIONS THEORY
Stephen McGlinchey, Rosie Walters & Dana Gold   1

PART ONE – ESTABLISHED THEORIES

1. REALISM
    Sandrina Antunes & Isabel Camisão   15

2. LIBERALISM
    Jeffrey W. Meiser   22

3. THE ENGLISH SCHOOL
    Yannis A. Stivachtis   28

4. CONSTRUCTIVISM
    Sarina Theys   36

5. MARXISM
    Maïa Pal   42

6. CRITICAL THEORY
    Marcos Farias Ferreira   49

7. POSTSTRUCTURALISM
    Aishling Mc Morrow   56

8. FEMINISM
    Sarah Smith   62

9. POSTCOLONIALISM
    Sheila Nair   69

10. TOWARDS A GLOBAL IR?
    Amitav Acharya   76

PART TWO – EXPANSION PACK

11. GREEN THEORY
     Hugh C. Dyer   84

12. GLOBAL JUSTICE
     Alix Dietzel   91

13. QUEER THEORY
     Markus Thiel   97

14. SECURITISATION THEORY
     Clara Eroukhmanoff   104

15. CRITICAL GEOGRAPHY
     Irena Leisbet Ceridwen Connon & Archie W. Simpson   110

16. ASIAN PERSPECTIVES
     Pichamon Yeophantong   117

17. GLOBAL SOUTH PERSPECTIVES
     Lina Benabdallah, Victor Adetula & Carlos Murillo-Zamora   125

18. INDIGENOUS PERSPECTIVES
     Jeff Corntassel & Marc Woons   131

19. A CONTEMPORARY PERSPECTIVE ON REALISM
     Felix Rösch & Richard Ned Lebow   138

20. THE 'ISMS' ARE EVIL. ALL HAIL THE 'ISMS'!
     Alex Prichard   145

REFERENCES   153

NOTE ON INDEXING   166

Contributors

Victor Adetula is Head of Research at the Nordic Africa Institute, Uppsala, Sweden and Professor of International Relations and Development Studies at the University of Jos, Nigeria.

Amitav Acharya is Distinguished Professor of International Relations and the UNESCO Chair in Transnational Challenges and Governance at American University, USA.

Sandrina Antunes is an Assistant Professor at the Department of International Relations and Public Administration at the Universidade do Minho, Portugal and a Scientific Fellow at the Center for the Study of Politics, Université Libre de Bruxelles, Belgium.

Lina Benabdallah is an Assistant Professor of Political Science at Wake Forest University, USA.

Isabel Camisão is an Assistant Professor of International Relations at the University of Évora, Portugal.

Irena Leisbet Ceridwen Connon is a Postdoctoral Research Fellow in Human Geography at the University of Dundee, UK.

Jeff Corntassel is an Associate Professor and Director of Indigenous Governance at the University of Victoria, Canada. He is a citizen of the Cherokee Nation.

Alix Dietzel is a Lecturer in Global Ethics at the University of Bristol, UK.

Hugh C. Dyer is an Associate Professor of World Politics at the University of Leeds, UK.

Clara Eroukhmanoff is a Lecturer in International Relations at London South Bank University, UK.

Marcos Farias Ferreira is a Lecturer in International Relations at the University of Lisbon and Instituto Universitário de Lisboa (ISCTE-IUL), Centro de Estudos Internacionais, Portugal.

Dana Gold is a PhD candidate at the University of Western Ontario in London, Canada.

Richard Ned Lebow is a Professor of International Political Theory at King's College London, UK, Bye-Fellow of Pembroke College, University of Cambridge, UK and the James O. Freedman Presidential Professor (Emeritus) of Government at Dartmouth College, USA.

Stephen McGlinchey is Senior Lecturer in International Relations at the University of the West of England, Bristol and Editor-in-Chief of E-International Relations.

Aishling Mc Morrow is a Lecturer in International Relations at Queen's University Belfast, UK.

Jeffrey W. Meiser is an Assistant Professor in Political Science at the University of Portland, USA.

Carlos Murillo-Zamora is a Professor at the University of Costa Rica and the National University of Costa Rica.

Sheila Nair is Professor of Politics and International Affairs at Northern Arizona University, USA.

Maïa Pal is a Senior Lecturer in International Relations at Oxford Brookes University, UK.

Alex Prichard is a Senior Lecturer in International Relations at the University of Exeter, UK.

Felix Rösch is a Senior Lecturer in International Relations at Coventry University, UK.

Christian Scheinpflug is Lead Editor of E-International Relations and a columnist at the *Santiago Times*.

Archie W. Simpson is a Teaching Fellow in Politics and International Relations at the University of Bath, UK.

Sarah Smith is visiting Assistant Professor in Gender Studies at Central European University, Budapest. She has also held lecturing posts at Monash University, Swinburne University of Technology and Australian Catholic University, Melbourne.

Yannis A. Stivachtis is an Associate Professor of Political Science and Director of the International Studies Program at Virginia Tech, USA.

Sarina Theys is a Contributing Lecturer in the Politics Department of Newcastle University, UK.

Markus Thiel is an Associate Professor of Politics & International Relations and Director of the EU/Jean Monnet Center of Excellence at Florida International University, USA.

Rosie Walters is a PhD candidate at the University of Bristol, UK and an Editor-at-Large of E-International Relations.

Marc Woons is a Doctoral Fellow with the Fonds Wetenschappelijk Onderzoek – Vlaanderen (Research Foundation – Flanders) and the Research in Political Philosophy Leuven (RIPPLE) Institute at the University of Leuven in Belgium.

Pichamon Yeophantong is a Lecturer in International Relations and Development at the University of New South Wales (UNSW Sydney), Australia.

Getting Started with International Relations Theory

STEPHEN MCGLINCHEY, ROSIE WALTERS & DANA GOLD

Before we go forward you should know that this book is available in e-book, PDF, web and paperback versions. While we know that many will use the digital versions of the book, we encourage you to buy a paperback copy as well if you are able. A growing body of research offers strong evidence that it is more effective to study from paper sources than from digital. Regardless of how you engage with the book, we hope it is an enjoyable read.

You can order the paperback version of this book in all good bookstores – from Amazon right down to your local bookstore – and digital versions are always freely available on the E-International Relations Students Portal: http://www.e-ir.info/students/

The Students Portal also includes a range of online resources that complement and expand upon the material in this book: http://www.e-ir.info/online-resources/

Hello

This book is designed as a foundational entry point to International Relations (IR) theory. As a beginner's guide, it has been structured to condense the most important information into the smallest space and present that information in the most accessible manner in order to introduce this area of study in a fresh way. It is recommended that you first consult this book's companion text *International Relations* (McGlinchey 2017) so that you have a fuller understanding of the discipline of International Relations before you delve into IR theory, which is one of its more difficult elements.

Theories of IR allow us to understand and try to make sense of the world around us through various lenses, each of which represents a different theoretical perspective. They are ways to simplify a complicated world. In a familiar analogy, theories are like maps. Each map is made for a certain purpose and what is included in the map is based on what is necessary to direct the map's user. All other details are left out to avoid confusion and present a clear picture. Since a picture paints a thousand words, go to Google and type in 'Singapore MRT' and then click on images. There you will see a map of Singapore's Mass Rapid Transit network. Enlarge it and stare at it for a moment. What you see there are lines, stations and some basic access information. You will not see public toilets, roads, banks, shops (and the like) charted as these are not essential to travelling on the system. Theories do a similar thing. Each different theory of IR puts different things on its map, based on what its theorists believe to be important. Variables to plot on an IR map would be such things as states, organisations, people, economics, history, ideas, class, gender and so on. Theorists then use their chosen variables to construct a simplified view of the world that can be used to analyse events – and in some cases to have a degree of predictive ability. In a practical sense, IR theories can be best seen as an analytical toolkit as they provide multiple methods for students to use to answer questions.

Some students love studying IR theories because they open up interesting questions about the world we live in, our understanding of human nature and even what it is possible to know. Some students, however, are eager to get straight to the real-life (often described as 'empirical') case studies of world events that made them want to study IR in the first place. For these students, studying IR theory might even seem like a distraction. Yet it is crucial to point out that embarking on the study of International Relations without an understanding of theory is like setting off on a journey without a map. You might arrive at your destination, or somewhere else very interesting, but you will have no idea where you are or how you got there. And you will have no response to someone who insists that their route would have been much better or more direct. Theories give us clarity and direction; they help us to both defend our own arguments and better understand the arguments of others.

This book presents a wide range of IR theories, split into two sections. The first section covers the established theories that are most commonly taught in undergraduate IR programmes. The second section expands to present emerging approaches and offer wider perspectives on IR theory. By giving equal space to the two sections we encourage readers to appreciate the diversity of IR theory. Each chapter of the book has a simple set of aims in mind. First, to compress and simplify the basics of each theory. Although theories are complex, our aim with this book is to provide an accessible foundation for further study rather than try to survey an entire field of scholarship. To return to the map analogy from above, our aim with each chapter is to give you a starting point on your journey – you will have to read deeper and wider to fully appreciate each theory's complexity. Like a good map, the chapters signpost you to where you can find this literature. Second, and to help you continue your journey in IR theory, each chapter also presents a case study of a real-world event or issue. This allows you to see each theory in action as a tool of analysis and understand the insights that IR theory can bring. The final chapter of each of the two sections (chapters 10 and 20) breaks this format and instead offers an innovative perspective on IR theory as a whole – allowing you to take a fresh view of things and reflect back on the discipline as you reach the mid and end points of the book.

Unlike most other textbooks, there are no boxes, charts, pictures or exercises included. The philosophy underpinning this book is that these things can be a distraction. This book, like others in the E-IR Foundations series, is designed to capture attention with an engaging narrative.

Before we get started, one very important note. You may notice that some of the theories you are introduced to here are referred to by names that also occur in other disciplines. They may be related to those theories, or not related at all. This can sometimes be confusing – for example, realism in IR is not the same as realism in art. Similarly, you may hear the word 'liberal' being used to describe someone's personal views, but in IR liberalism means something quite distinct. To avoid any confusion, this note will serve as a caveat that in this book we refer to the theories concerned only as they have been developed within the discipline of International Relations. Where minor exceptions to this rule are necessary, this will be stated clearly to avoid reader confusion.

A brief introduction to IR theory

As international relations has grown in complexity, the family of theories that IR offers has grown in number, which presents a challenge for newcomers to IR theory. However, this introduction should give you the confidence to get started. To kick off, this section will briefly introduce IR theory via a three-part spectrum of traditional theories, middle ground theories and critical theories. As you read further into the book, you should expect this simple three-part picture to dissolve somewhat – though it is a useful device to come back to should you get confused.

Theories are constantly emerging and competing with one another. This can be disorientating. As soon as you think you have found your feet with one theoretical approach, others appear. This section will therefore serve as both a primer and a warning that complexity is to be expected ahead! Even though this book presents IR theory in a particularly simple and basic way, complexity remains. IR theory requires your full attention and you should buckle down and expect turbulence on your journey.

Thomas Kuhn's *The Structure of Scientific Revolutions* (1962) set the stage for understanding how and why certain theories are legitimised and widely accepted. He also identified the process that takes place when theories are no longer relevant and new theories emerge. For example, human beings were once convinced that the earth was flat. With the advancement of science and technology, there was a significant discovery and humans discarded this belief. When such a discovery takes place, a 'paradigm shift' results and the former way of thinking is replaced by a new one. Although changes in IR theory are not as dramatic as the example above, there have been significant evolutions in the discipline. This is important to keep in mind when we consider how theories of IR play a role in explaining the world and how, based upon different time periods and our personal contexts, one approach may speak to us more than another.

All of the theories previewed in this section (and many more besides) are covered in their own chapters in the book.

Traditionally there have been two central theories of IR: liberalism and realism. Although they have come under great challenge from other theories, they remain central to the discipline. At its height, liberalism was referred to as a 'utopian' theory and to some degree is still recognised as such today. Its proponents view human beings as innately good and believe peace and harmony between nations is not only achievable, but desirable. In the late eighteenth century, Immanuel Kant developed the idea that states that shared liberal values should have no reason for going to war against one another. In Kant's eyes, the more liberal states there were in the world, the more peaceful it would become, since liberal states are ruled by their citizens and citizens are rarely disposed to go to war. This is in contrast to the rule of kings and other non-elected rulers who frequently have selfish desires out of step with citizens. His ideas have resonated and continue to be developed by modern liberals, most notably in the democratic peace theory, which posits that democracies do not go to war with each other.

Further, liberals have faith in the idea that the permanent cessation of war is an attainable goal. Putting liberal ideas into practice, US President Woodrow Wilson addressed his 'Fourteen Points' to the US Congress in January 1918 during the final year of the First World War. The last of his 'points' – ideas for a rebuilt world beyond the war – was the setting up of a general association of nations: this became the League of Nations. Dating back to 1920, the League of Nations was created largely for the purpose of overseeing affairs between states and implementing, as well as maintaining, international peace. However, when the League collapsed due to the outbreak of the Second World War in 1939, its failure was difficult for liberals to comprehend, as events seemed to contradict their theories. Therefore, despite the efforts of figures such as Kant and Wilson, liberalism failed to retain a strong hold and a new theory emerged to explain the continuing presence of war. That theory became known as realism.

Realism gained momentum during the Second World War, when it appeared to offer a convincing account for how and why the most widespread and deadly war in known history followed a period of supposed peace and optimism. Although it originated in named form in the twentieth century, many realists look back much further. Indeed, realists have looked as far back as the ancient world, where they detected similar patterns of human behaviour as those evident in our modern world. As its name suggests, advocates of realism purport that it reflects the 'reality' of the world and more effectively accounts for change in international politics. Thomas Hobbes is often mentioned in discussions of realism due to his description of the brutality of life during the English Civil War of 1642–1651. Hobbes described human beings as living in an orderless 'state of nature' that he perceived as a war of all against all. To remedy this, he proposed a 'social contract' between the ruler and the people of a state to maintain relative order. Today, we take such ideas for granted as it is usually clear who rules our states. Each leader, or 'sovereign' (a monarch or a parliament, for example), sets the rules and establishes a system of punishments for those who break them. We accept this in our respective states so that our lives can function with a sense of security and order. It may not be ideal, but it is better than a state of nature. As no such contract exists internationally and there is no sovereign in charge of the world, disorder and fear rules international relations. For realists, we live in a system of 'international anarchy'. That is why war seems more common than peace to realists; indeed, they see it as inevitable.

It is important to understand that, despite what the layout of the chapters in this book may suggest, there is no single variant of each theory. Scholars rarely fully agree with each other, even those who share the same theoretical approach. Each scholar has a particular interpretation of the world, which includes ideas of peace, war and the role of the state in relation to individuals. Nevertheless, these perspectives can still be grouped into theory families (or traditions) and this is how we have organised the material in this book. In your studies you will need to unpack the various differences but, for now, understanding the core assumptions of each approach is the best way to get your bearings. For example, if we think of the simple contrast of optimism and pessimism we can see a familial relationship in all branches of realism and liberalism. Liberals share an optimistic view of IR, believing that world order can be improved, with peace and progress gradually replacing war. They may not agree on the details, but this optimistic view generally unites them. Conversely, realists tend to dismiss optimism as a form of misplaced idealism and instead they arrive at a more pessimistic view. This is due to their focus on the centrality of the state and its need for security and survival in an anarchical system where it can only truly rely on itself. As a result, realists reach an array of accounts that describe IR as a system where war and conflict is common and periods of peace are merely times when states are preparing for future conflict.

The thinking of the English school is often viewed as a middle ground between liberal and realist theories. Its theory involves the idea of a society of states existing at the international level. Hedley Bull, one of the core figures of the English school, agreed with traditional theories that the international system was anarchic. However, he insisted this does not mean the absence of norms (expected behaviours), thus claiming a societal aspect to international politics. In this sense, states form an 'Anarchical Society' (Bull 1977) where a type of order does exist, based on shared norms and behaviours.

Constructivism is another theory commonly viewed as a middle ground, but this time between mainstream theories and the critical theories that we will explore later. It also has some familial links with the English school. Unlike scholars from other perspectives, constructivists highlight the importance of values and of shared interests between individuals who interact on the global stage. Alexander Wendt, a prominent constructivist, described the relationship between agents (individuals) and structures (such as the state) as one in which structures not only constrain agents but also construct their identities and interests. His phrase 'anarchy is what states make of it' (Wendt 1992) sums this up well. Another way to explain this, and to explain the core of constructivism, is that the essence of international relations exists in the interactions between people. After all, states do not interact; it is agents of those states, such as politicians and diplomats, who interact. Since those interacting on the world stage have accepted international anarchy as its defining principle, it has become part of our reality. However, if anarchy is what we make of it, then different states can perceive anarchy differently and the qualities of anarchy can even change over time. International anarchy could even be replaced by a different system if an influential group of other individuals (and by proxy the states they represent) accepted the idea. To understand constructivism is to understand that ideas, or 'norms' as they are often called, have power. As such, constructivists seek to study the process by which norms are challenged and potentially replaced with new norms.

Critical approaches refer to a wide spectrum of theories that have been established in response to mainstream approaches in the field, mainly liberalism and realism. In a nutshell, critical theorists share one particular trait – they oppose commonly held assumptions in the field of IR that have been central since its establishment. They call for new approaches that are better suited to understand, as well as question, the world we find ourselves in. Critical theories are valuable because they identify positions that have typically been ignored or overlooked within IR. They also give a voice to groups of people who have frequently been marginalised, particularly women and those from the Global South. Much of this book's expansion pack deals with theories set within this larger category.

Marxism is a good place to start with critical theories. This approach is based upon the ideas of Karl Marx, who lived in the nineteenth century at the height of the industrial revolution. The term 'Marxist' refers to people who have adopted Marx's views and believe that industrialised society is divided into two classes – the business class of 'owners' (the bourgeoisie) and the working class (the proletariat). The proletariat are at the mercy of the bourgeoisie who control their wages and therefore their standard of living. Marx hoped for the overthrow of the bourgeoisie by the proletariat and an eventual end to the class society. Critical theorists who take a Marxist angle often argue that the organisation of international politics around the state has led to ordinary people around the globe becoming divided and alienated, instead of recognising what they all have in common – potentially – as a global proletariat. For this to change, the legitimacy of the state must be questioned and ultimately dissolved. In that sense, emancipation from the state in some form is often part of the wider critical agenda.

Postcolonialism differs from Marxism by focusing on the inequality between nations or regions, as opposed to classes. The effects of colonialism are still felt in many regions of the world today as local populations continue to deal with the challenges created and left behind by ex-colonial powers such as the United Kingdom and France. Postcolonialism's origins can be traced to the Cold War period when much activity in international relations centred around decolonisation and the wish to undo the legacies of European imperialism. This approach acknowledges that the study of IR has historically centred on Western perspectives and experiences, excluding the voices of people from other regions of the world. Crucially, postcolonial scholars have argued that analyses based on Western theoretical perspectives, or that do not take into account the perspectives of those in former colonies, may lead international institutions and world leaders to take actions that unfairly favour the West. They have created a deeper understanding of the way in which the operations of the global economy, the decision-making processes of international institutions and the actions of the great powers might actually constitute new forms of colonialism. Edward Said's (1978) *Orientalism* described how societies in the Middle East and Asia were regularly misrepresented in Western literary and scholarly writing in a way that positioned them as inferior to the West. Postcolonial scholars are, therefore, important contributors to the field as they widen the focus of enquiry beyond IR's traditionally 'Western' mindset.

Another theory that exposes the inequality inherent in international relations is feminism. Feminism entered the field in the 1980s as part of the emerging critical movement. It focused on explaining why so few women seemed to be in positions of power and examining the implications of this on how global politics was structured. You only need look at a visual of any meeting of world leaders to see how it appears to be a man's world. Recognising this introduces a 'gendered' reading of IR, where we place an issue such as gender as the prime object on our map. If it is a man's world, what does that mean? How have certain characteristics traditionally viewed as masculine – such as aggression, emotional detachment and strength – come to be seen as essential qualities of a world leader? Which qualities and characteristics does this exclude (it might be empathy and cooperation) and what kind of actions does this result in? By recognising that gender – the roles that society constructs for men and women – permeates everything, feminism challenges those roles in a way that benefits everyone. It is not simply a question of counting male and female bodies. Rather, feminists ask how gendered power structures make it difficult for women or men who display supposedly feminine traits to reach the highest levels of power. Given that those positions involve making life and death decisions, it matters to all of us whether the person who gets there is known for their aggression or their compassion. With all this talk of socially constructed gender roles, you might be beginning to see some overlaps – with constructivism, for example. We are doing our best to present each approach separately so that you have a clearer starting point, but it is wise to caution you that IR theory is a dense and complex web and not always clearly defined. Keep this in mind as you read on and as your studies develop.

Perhaps the most controversial of the critical theories is poststructuralism. This is an approach that questions the very beliefs we have all come to know and feel as 'real'. Poststructuralism questions the dominant narratives that have been widely accepted by mainstream theories. For instance, liberals and realists both accept the idea of the state and for the most part take it for granted. Such assumptions are foundational 'truths' on which those traditional theories rest – becoming 'structures' that they build their account of reality around. So, although these two theoretical perspectives may differ in some respects with regard to their overall worldviews, they share a general understanding of the world. Neither theory seeks to challenge the existence of the state; they simply count it as part of their reality. Poststructuralism seeks to question these commonly held assumptions of reality, not just the state but also more widely the nature of power. Michel Foucault's contribution to poststructuralism was his identification of the knowledge–power nexus. What this means is that people in a position of power, including politicians, journalists, even scholars, have the ability to shape our common understandings of a given issue. In turn, these understandings of the issue can become so ingrained that they appear to be common sense and it becomes difficult to think outside of them, leaving room for only certain kinds of action. Power is knowledge and knowledge is power. By analysing the way in which a certain understanding of an issue becomes dominant, poststructuralists aim to expose the hidden assumptions it is based upon. They also aim to open up other possible ways of being, thinking and doing in international politics.

As this brief introduction to IR theory has shown, each theory of IR possesses a legitimate, yet different, view of the world. Indeed, beyond the theories explored above are many other theories and perspectives that you will find in the expansion pack section of this book. It is also important to note that the theories covered in this book are not exhaustive and there are more that could be examined. However, the book's editors believe that we have provided a good starting point for achieving an overall understanding of the field and where the most common, and most novel, approaches and perspectives are situated. It is not necessary – and probably not wise so early in your studies – to adopt one theory as your own. It is more important to understand the various theories as tools of analysis, or analytical lenses, that you can apply in your studies. Simply, they offer a means by which to attempt to understand a complex world.

Thinking like a scholar

Since studying IR theory requires real focus, you should start to consider how to make the space and time to concentrate as you read this book. You will need to put your devices on silent, close your internet browsers and find a quiet space to work. Take ten-minute mini-breaks every hour or so to do other things and make sure to eat a decent meal midway through your study session to give you a longer break. Finally, try to get a good night's sleep before and after you study. Your brain does not absorb or retain information very well when you are sleep deprived or hungry. There will be times in the year when panic sets in as deadlines approach, but if you have already developed a good reading strategy you will find you are in good shape for the task at hand. So, before we delve further into IR theory, we will try to give you some tips to help you think like a scholar.

Reading for scholarly purposes is not the same as reading for pleasure. You need to adopt a reading strategy. Everyone has their own way of doing this, but the basic tip is this: *take notes as you read*. If you find that you don't have many notes or your mind goes a little blank, then you might be reading too quickly or not paying enough attention. This is most likely if you are reading digitally on a computer or tablet, as it is very easy for eyes to wander or for you to drift onto a social media site. If this happens, don't worry: just go back and start again. Often, reading something a second time is when it clicks.

Best practice is to make rough notes as you read through each chapter. When you get to the end of a chapter, compile your rough notes into a list of 'key points' that you would like to remember. This will be useful when you come to revise or recap an issue because you won't necessarily have to read the entire chapter again. Your notes should trigger your memory and remind you of the key information. Some textbooks do this for you and provide a list of key points at the end of each chapter. This book, being a foundational book for beginners, does *not* do so: we want readers to develop the important skills of reading and note-taking for themselves and not take short cuts.

Although there is no substitute for reading, if you find a certain theory is not clicking, go to the online resources section of the E-IR Student Portal (linked below) and you will find carefully selected audio and visual resources on each theory to give yourself a different perspective: http://www.e-ir.info/online-resources-international-relations-theory/

By making notes on everything you encounter you will form a strategy that will allow you to retain the most important information and compress it into a smaller set of notes integral to revision for examinations or preparation for discussions and assignments. It's best to use digital means (laptop/tablet) so you can create backups and not risk losing valuable handwritten paper notes. If you do use paper notes, take pictures of them on your phone so you have a backup just in case.

You should also note down the citation information for each set of notes at the top of the page so that you can identify the source you took the notes from if you need to reference it later in any written work. As theories are most often developed in written form it is important to understand how to properly reference the work of theorists as you encounter them. Referencing sources is very important in academia. It is the way scholars and students attribute the work of others, whether they use their exact words or not. For that reason it is usual to see numerous references in the expert literature you will progress to after completing this book. It is an important element of scholarly writing, and one that you should master for your own studies. In this book we have tried to summarise issues from an expert perspective so as to give you an uninterrupted narrative. When we need to point you to more specialist literature, for example to invite you to read a little deeper, we do so by inserting in-text citations that look like this: (Hutchings 2001). These point you to a corresponding entry in the references section towards the back of the book where you can find the full reference and follow it up if you want to. Typically, these are books, journal articles or websites. In-text citations always include the author's surname and the year of publication. As the reference list is organised alphabetically by surname, you can quickly locate the full reference. Sometimes you will also find page numbers inside the brackets. For example, (Hutchings 2001, 11–13). Page numbers are added when referring to specific arguments, or a quotation, from a source. This referencing system is known as the 'Author-Date' or 'Harvard' system. It is the most common, but not the only, referencing system used in IR.

When the time comes for you to make your own arguments and write your own assignments, think of using sources as if you were a lawyer preparing a court case. Your task there would be to convince a jury that your argument is defensible, beyond reasonable doubt. You would have to present clear, well-organised evidence based on facts and expertise. If you presented evidence that was just someone's uninformed opinion, the jury would not find it convincing and you would lose the case. Similarly, in academic writing you have to make sure that the sources you use are reputable. You can usually find this out by looking up the author and the publisher. If the author is not an expert (academic, practitioner, etc.) and/or the publisher is unknown/obscure, then the source is likely unreliable. It may have interesting information, but it is not reputable by scholarly standards.

It should be safe to assume that you know what a book is (since you are reading one!) and that you understand what the internet is. However, one type of source that you will find cited in this book and may not have encountered before is the journal article. Journal articles are typically only accessible from your university library as they are expensive and require a subscription. They are papers prepared by academics, for academics. As such, they represent the latest thinking and may contain cutting-edge insights. But, they are often complex and dense due to their audience being fellow experts, which makes them hard for a beginner to read. In addition, journal articles are peer reviewed. This means they have gone through a process of assessment by other experts before being published. During that process many changes and improvements may be made – and articles often fail to make it through peer review and are rejected. So, journal articles are something of a gold standard in scholarly writing.

Most journal articles are now available on the internet, which leads to confusion as students can find it difficult to distinguish a journal article from an online magazine or newspaper article. Works of journalism or opinion are not peer reviewed and conform to different professional standards. If you follow the tip above and 'search' the publisher and author, you should be able to discern which is which. Another helpful tip is length. A journal article will typically be 10–20 pages long (7,000–11,000 words); articles of journalism or commentary will usually be shorter.

A final note on the subject of sources: the internet is something of a Wild West. There is great information there, but also a lot of rubbish. It can often be hard to tell them apart. But, again, if you follow the golden rule of looking up the author and looking up the publisher (using the internet), you can usually find your way. However, even some of the world's biggest websites can be unreliable. Wikipedia, for example, is a great resource, but it often has incorrect information because it is authored, and usually edited, by ordinary people who are typically enthusiasts rather than experts. In addition, its pages are always changing (because of user edits), making it hard to rely on as a source. So the rule of thumb with the internet is to try to corroborate anything you find on at least two good websites/from at least two reputable authors. Then you can use the internet with confidence and enjoy its benefits while avoiding its pitfalls. When preparing assignments, however, you should only use the internet to supplement the more robust information you will find in academic journals and books.

Another important part of learning to think like a scholar is to understand the language that scholars use. Each discipline has its own unique language. This comprises a range of specific terms that have been developed by scholars to describe certain things. As a result, a lot of the time you spend learning a discipline is spent learning its jargon so that you can access and understand the literature. Instead of packing this book with jargon we have tried as far as possible to explain things in ordinary language while easing you into the more peculiar terminology found within IR theory. This approach should keep you engaged while giving you the confidence to read the more advanced literature that you will soon encounter.

Understanding key terms even applies to something as basic as how to express the term 'International Relations'. The academic convention is to capitalise it (International Relations, abbreviated as 'IR') when referring to the academic discipline – that is, the subject taught in university campuses all over the world. IR does not describe events; rather, it is a scholarly discipline that seeks to *understand* events – with IR theory being a major tool in that endeavour. On the other hand, 'international relations' – not capitalised – is generally used by both scholars and non-scholars to *describe* relations between states, organisations and individuals at the global level. This term is interchangeable with terms such as 'global politics', 'world politics' or 'international politics'. They all mean pretty much the same thing. We have maintained this capitalisation convention in the book.

We should also mention that as this book is published in the UK it is presented in British English. This means words like 'globalisation' and 'organisation' are spelt with an 's' rather than a 'z'.

Bottom line

All theories are imperfect. If one was accurate at accounting for behaviour and actions in IR, there would be no need for any others. The sheer volume of different IR theories should be a warning to you that International Relations still is a young discipline that is undergoing significant formative development. Within that development is a sometimes fierce set of arguments over the nature of the state, the individual, international organisations, identity and even reality itself. The important point to remember is that theories are tools of analysis. Often they are pertinent and insightful when applied correctly to understand an event. But just as often they are imperfect and you will find yourself reaching for a more applicable theoretical tool. This book will equip you with a foundational starting point for developing your own IR theory toolkit, so that no matter what your task, you are armed with all that you need to get started in your analysis and well oriented to access – and understand – the key texts and more advanced textbooks within the field. Good luck!

Part One

ESTABLISHED THEORIES

1

Realism

SANDRINA ANTUNES & ISABEL CAMISÃO

In the discipline of International Relations (IR), realism is a school of thought that emphasises the competitive and conflictual side of international relations. Realism's roots are often said to be found in some of humankind's earliest historical writings, particularly Thucydides' history of the Peloponnesian War, which raged between 431 and 404 BCE. Thucydides, writing over two thousand years ago, was not a 'realist' because IR theory did not exist in named form until the twentieth century. However, when looking back from a contemporary vantage point, theorists detected many similarities in the thought patterns and behaviours of the ancient world and the modern world. They then drew on his writings, and that of others, to lend weight to the idea that there was a timeless theory spanning all recorded human history. That theory was named 'realism'.

The basics of realism

The first assumption of realism is that the nation-state (usually abbreviated to 'state') is the principle actor in international relations. Other bodies exist, such as individuals and organisations, but their power is limited. Second, the state is a unitary actor. National interests, especially in times of war, lead the state to speak and act with one voice. Third, decision-makers are rational actors in the sense that rational decision-making leads to the pursuit of the national interest. Here, taking actions that would make your state weak or vulnerable would not be rational. Realism suggests that all leaders, no matter what their political persuasion, recognise this as they attempt to manage their state's affairs in order to survive in a competitive environment. Finally, states live in a context of anarchy – that is, in the absence of anyone being in charge internationally. The often-used analogy of there being 'no one to call' in an international emergency helps to underline this point. Within our own states we typically have police forces, militaries, courts and so on. In an emergency, there is an expectation that these institutions will 'do something' in response.

Internationally, there is no clear expectation of anyone or anything 'doing something' as there is no established hierarchy. Therefore, states can ultimately only rely on themselves.

As realism frequently draws on examples from the past, there is a great deal of emphasis on the idea that humans are essentially held hostage to repetitive patterns of behaviour determined by their nature. Central to that assumption is the view that human beings are egoistic and desire power. Realists believe that our selfishness, our appetite for power and our inability to trust others leads to predictable outcomes. Perhaps this is why war has been so common throughout recorded history. Since individuals are organised into states, human nature impacts on state behaviour. In that respect, Niccolò Machiavelli focused on how the basic human characteristics influence the security of the state. And in his time, leaders were usually male, which also influences the realist account of politics. In *The Prince* (1532), Machiavelli stressed that a leader's primary concern is to promote national security. In order to successfully perform this task, the leader needs to be alert and cope effectively with internal as well as external threats to his rule; he needs to be a lion and a fox. Power (the Lion) and deception (the Fox) are crucial tools for the conduct of foreign policy. In Machiavelli's view, rulers obey the 'ethics of responsibility' rather than the conventional religious morality that guides the average citizen – that is, they should be good when they can, but they must also be willing to use violence when necessary to guarantee the survival of the state.

In the aftermath of the Second World War, Hans Morgenthau (1948) sought to develop a comprehensive international theory as he believed that politics, like society in general, is governed by laws that have roots in human nature. His concern was to clarify the relationship between interests and morality in international politics, and his work drew heavily on the insights of historical figures such as Thucydides and Machiavelli. In contrast to more optimistically minded idealists who expected international tensions to be resolved through open negotiations marked by goodwill, Morgenthau set out an approach that emphasised power over morality. Indeed, morality was portrayed as something that should be avoided in policymaking. In Morgenthau's account, every political action is directed towards keeping, increasing or demonstrating power. The thinking is that policies based on morality or idealism can lead to weakness – and possibly the destruction or domination of a state by a competitor. In this sense pursuing the national interest is 'amoral' – meaning that it is not subject to calculations of morality.

In *Theory of International Politics* (1979), Kenneth Waltz modernised IR theory by moving realism away from its unprovable (albeit persuasive) assumptions about human nature. His theoretical contribution was termed 'neorealism' or 'structural realism' because he emphasised the notion of 'structure' in his explanation. Rather than a state's decisions and actions being based on human nature, they are arrived at via a simple formula. First, all states are constrained by existing in an international anarchic system (this is the structure). Second, any course of action they pursue is based on their relative power when measured against other states. So, Waltz offered a version of realism that recommended that theorists examine the characteristics of the international system for answers rather than delve into flaws in human nature. In doing so, he sparked a new era in IR theory that attempted to use social scientific methods rather than political theory (or philosophical) methods. The difference is that Waltz's variables (international anarchy, how much power a state has, etc.) can be empirically/physically measured. Ideas like human nature are assumptions based on certain philosophical views that cannot be measured in the same way.

Realists believe that their theory most closely describes the image of world politics held by practitioners of statecraft. For this reason, realism, perhaps more than any other IR theory, is often utilised in the world of policymaking – echoing Machiavelli's desire to write a manual to guide leaders. However, realism's critics argue that realists can help perpetuate the violent and confrontational world that they describe. By assuming the uncooperative and egoistic nature of humankind and the absence of hierarchy in the state system, realists encourage leaders to act in ways based on suspicion, power and force. Realism can thus be seen as a self-fulfilling prophecy. More directly, realism is often criticised as excessively pessimistic, since it sees the confrontational nature of the international system as inevitable. However, according to realists, leaders are faced with endless constraints and few opportunities for cooperation. Thus, they can do little to escape the reality of power politics. For a realist, facing the reality of one's predicament is not pessimism – it is prudence. The realist account of international relations stresses that the possibility of peaceful change, or in fact any type of change, is limited. For a leader to rely on such an idealistic outcome would be folly.

Perhaps because it is designed to explain repetition and a timeless pattern of behaviour, realism was not able to predict or explain a major recent transformation of the international system: the end of the Cold War between the United States of America (US) and the Soviet Union in 1991. When the Cold War ended, international politics underwent rapid change that pointed to a new era of limited competition between states and abundant opportunities for cooperation. This transformation prompted the emergence of an optimistic vision of world politics that discarded realism as 'old thinking'. Realists are also accused of focusing too much on the state as a solid unit, ultimately overlooking other actors and forces within the state and also ignoring international issues not directly connected to the survival of the state. For example, the Cold War ended because ordinary citizens in Soviet-controlled nations in Eastern Europe decided to rebel against existing power structures. This rebellion swept from one country to another within the Soviet Union's vast empire, resulting in its gradual collapse between 1989 and 1991. Realism's toolbox did not and does not account for such events: the actions of ordinary citizens (or international organisations, for that matter) have no major part in its calculations. This is due to the state-centred nature of the thinking that realism is built upon. It views states as solid pool balls bouncing around a table – never stopping to look inside each pool ball to see what it comprises and why it moves the way it does. Realists recognise the importance of these criticisms, but tend to see events such as the collapse of the Soviet Union as exceptions to the normal pattern of things.

Many critics of realism focus on one of its central strategies in the management of world affairs – an idea called 'the balance of power'. This describes a situation in which states are continuously making choices to increase their own capabilities while undermining the capabilities of others. This generates a 'balance' of sorts as (theoretically) no state is permitted to get too powerful within the international system. If a state attempts to push its luck and grow too much, like Nazi Germany in the 1930s, it will trigger a war because other states will form an alliance to try to defeat it – that is, restore a balance. This balance of power system is one of the reasons why international relations is anarchic. No single state has been able to become a global power and unite the world under its direct rule. Hence, realism talks frequently about the importance of flexible alliances as a way of ensuring survival. These alliances are determined less by political or cultural similarities among states and more by the need to find fair-weather friends, or 'enemies of my enemy'. This may help to explain why the US and the Soviet Union were allied during the Second World War (1939–1945): they both saw a similar threat from a rising Germany and sought to balance it. Yet within a couple of years of the war ending, the nations had become bitter enemies and the balance of power started to shift again as new alliances were formed during what became known as the Cold War (1947–1991). While realists describe the balance of power as a prudent strategy to manage an insecure world, critics see it as a way of legitimising war and aggression.

Despite these criticisms, realism remains central within the field of IR theory, with most other theories concerned (at least in part) with critiquing it. For that reason, it would be inappropriate to write a textbook on IR theory without covering realism in the first chapter. In addition, realism continues to offer many important insights about the world of policymaking due to its history of offering tools of statecraft to policymakers.

Realism and the Islamic State Group

The Islamic State group (also known as IS, Daesh, ISIS or ISIL) is a militant group that follows a fundamentalist doctrine of Sunni Islam. In June 2014, the group published a document where it claimed to have traced the lineage of its leader, Abu Bakr al-Baghdadi, back to the prophet Muhammad. The group then appointed al-Baghdadi its 'caliph'. As caliph, al-Baghdadi demanded the allegiance of devout Muslims worldwide and the group and its supporters set about conducting a range of extreme and barbaric acts. Many of these were targeted at cities in Western nations such as Melbourne, Manchester and Paris – which has led to the issue becoming a global one. Ultimately, the intent is to create an Islamic State (or Caliphate) in geopolitical, cultural and political terms and to deter (via the use of terrorism and extreme actions) Western or regional powers from interfering with this process. Of course, this means that existing states' territory is under threat. Although the Islamic State group considers itself a state, due to its actions it has been defined as a terrorist organisation by virtually all of the world's states and international organisations. Islamic religious leaders have also condemned the group's ideology and actions.

Despite it not being an officially recognised state, by taking and holding territory in Iraq and Syria, the Islamic State group clearly possessed aspects of statehood. The major part of efforts to fight the Islamic State group has comprised airstrikes against its positions, combined with other military strategies such as using allied local forces to retake territory (most notably in Iraq). This suggests that war is considered the most effective method of counterbalancing the increasing power of terrorism in the Middle East and neutralising the threat that the Islamic State group poses not only to Western states but also to states in the region. So, while transnational terrorism, such as that practised by the Islamic State group, is a relatively new threat in international relations, states have relied on old strategies consistent with realism to deal with it.

States ultimately count on self-help for guaranteeing their own security. Within this context, realists have two main strategies for managing insecurity: the balance of power and deterrence. The balance of power relies on strategic, flexible alliances, while deterrence relies on the threat (or the use) of significant force. Both are in evidence in this case. First, the loose coalition of states that attacked the Islamic State group – states such as the US, Russia and France – relied on various fair-weather alliances with regional powers such as Saudi Arabia, Turkey and Iran. At the same time, they downplayed the role of international organisations because agreeing action in places such as the United Nations is difficult due to state rivalry. Second, deterring an enemy with overwhelming, superior force (or the threat of it) was perceived as the quickest method to regain control over the territories under Islamic State's rule. The obvious disproportionality of Islamic State's military forces when compared with the military forces of the US, France or Russia seems to confirm the rationality of the decision – which again harks back to realism's emphasis on the importance of concepts like deterrence, but also on viewing states as rational actors. However, the rational actor approach presupposes that the enemy – even if a terrorist group – is also a rational actor who would choose a course of action in which the benefits outweigh the risks.

Via this point, we can see that while the actions of a terrorist group might appear irrational, they can be interpreted otherwise. From a realist perspective, the Islamic State group, by spreading terror, is using the limited means at its disposal to counterbalance Western influence in Iraq and Syria. The substantial collateral damage of a full military offensive is evidently not a concern for the group's commanders for two main reasons, both of which may serve to enhance their power. First, it would contribute to fuelling anti-Western sentiment throughout the Middle East as local populations become the target of foreign aggression. Second, the feeling of injustice prompted by these attacks creates an opportunity for the spontaneous recruitment of fighters who would be willing to die to validate the group's aims – this is equally true for those within the immediate region and those internationally who fall prey to Islamic State propaganda on the internet.

It is for reasons such as those unpacked in this case, in regions that are as complex as the Middle East, that realists recommend extreme caution regarding when and where a state uses its military power. It is easy when viewing realism to see it as a warmongering theory. For example, on reading the first half of the paragraph above you might feel that realism would support an attack on the Islamic State group. But when you read the second half of the paragraph you will find that the same theory recommends extreme caution.

The key point in understanding realism is that it is a theory that argues that unsavoury actions like war are necessary tools of statecraft in an imperfect world and leaders must use them when it is in the national interest. This is wholly rational in a world where the survival of the state is pre-eminent. After all, if one's state ceases to exist due to attack or internal collapse, then all other political objectives cease to have much practical relevance. That being said, a leader must be extremely cautious when deciding where and when to use military power. It is worth noting that the US invasion of Iraq in 2003, undertaken as part of the Global War on Terror, was opposed by most leading realists as a misuse of power that would not serve US national interests. This was due to the possibility that the disproportionate use of US military force would cause blowback and resentment in the region. Indeed, in this case, realism yielded strong results as a tool of analysis, as the rise of the Islamic State group in the years after the Iraq invasion demonstrated.

Conclusion

Realism is a theory that claims to explain the *reality* of international politics. It emphasises the constraints on politics that result from humankind's egoistic nature and the absence of a central authority above the state. For realists, the highest goal is the survival of the state, which explains why states' actions are judged according to the ethics of responsibility rather than by moral principles. The dominance of realism has generated a significant strand of literature criticising its main tenets. However, despite the value of the criticisms, which will be explored in the rest of this book, realism continues to provide valuable insights and remains an important analytical tool for every student of International Relations.

2

Liberalism

JEFFREY W. MEISER

Liberalism is a defining feature of modern democracy, illustrated by the prevalence of the term 'liberal democracy' as a way to describe countries with free and fair elections, rule of law and protected civil liberties. However, liberalism – when discussed within the realm of IR theory – has evolved into a distinct entity of its own. Liberalism contains a variety of concepts and arguments about how institutions, behaviours and economic connections contain and mitigate the violent power of states. When compared to realism, it adds more factors into our field of view – especially a consideration of citizens and international organisations. Most notably, liberalism has been the traditional foil of realism in IR theory as it offers a more optimistic world view, grounded in a different reading of history to that found in realist scholarship.

The basics of liberalism

Liberalism is based on the moral argument that ensuring the right of an individual person to life, liberty and property is the highest goal of government. Consequently, liberals emphasise the wellbeing of the individual as the fundamental building block of a just political system. A political system characterised by unchecked power, such as a monarchy or a dictatorship, cannot protect the life and liberty of its citizens. Therefore, the main concern of liberalism is to construct institutions that protect individual freedom by limiting and checking political power. While these are issues of domestic politics, the realm of IR is also important to liberals because a state's activities abroad can have a strong influence on liberty at home. Liberals are particularly troubled by militaristic foreign policies. The primary concern is that war requires states to build up military power. This power can be used for fighting foreign states, but it can also be used to oppress its own citizens. For this reason, political systems rooted in liberalism often limit military power by such means as ensuring civilian control over the military.

Wars of territorial expansion, or imperialism – when states seek to build empires by taking territory overseas – are especially disturbing for liberals. Not only do expansionist wars strengthen the state at the expense of the people, these wars also require long-term commitments to the military occupation and political control of foreign territory and peoples. Occupation and control require large bureaucracies that have an interest in maintaining or expanding the occupation of foreign territory. For liberals, therefore, the core problem is how to develop a political system that can allow states to protect themselves from foreign threats without subverting the individual liberty of its citizenry. The primary institutional check on power in liberal states is free and fair elections via which the people can remove their rulers from power, providing a fundamental check on the behaviour of the government. A second important limitation on political power is the division of political power among different branches and levels of government – such as a parliament/congress, an executive and a legal system. This allows for checks and balances in the use of power.

Democratic peace theory is perhaps the strongest contribution liberalism makes to IR theory. It asserts that democratic states are highly unlikely to go to war with one another. There is a two-part explanation for this phenomenon. First, democratic states are characterised by internal restraints on power, as described above. Second, democracies tend to see each other as legitimate and unthreatening and therefore have a higher capacity for cooperation with each other than they do with non-democracies. Statistical analysis and historical case studies provide strong support for democratic peace theory, but several issues continue to be debated. First, democracy is a relatively recent development in human history. This means there are few cases of democracies having the opportunity to fight one another. Second, we cannot be sure whether it is truly a 'democratic' peace or whether some other factors correlated with democracy are the source of peace – such as power, alliances, culture, economics and so on. A third point is that while democracies are unlikely to go to war with one another, some scholarship suggests that they are likely to be aggressive toward non-democracies – such as when the United States went to war with Iraq in 2003. Despite the debate, the possibility of a democratic peace gradually replacing a world of constant war – as described by realists – is an enduring and important facet of liberalism.

We currently live in an international system structured by the liberal world order built after the Second World War (1939–1945). The international institutions, organisations and norms (expected behaviours) of this world order are built on the same foundations as domestic liberal institutions and norms; the desire to restrain the violent power of states. Yet, power is more diluted and dispersed internationally than it is within states. For example, under international law, wars of aggression are prohibited. There is no international police force to enforce this law, but an aggressor knows that when breaking this law it risks considerable international backlash. For example, states – either individually or as part of a collective body like the United Nations – can impose economic sanctions or intervene militarily against the offending state. Furthermore, an aggressive state also risks missing out on the benefits of peace, such as the gains from international trade, foreign aid and diplomatic recognition.

The fullest account of the liberal world order is found in the work of Daniel Deudney and G. John Ikenberry (1999), who describe three interlocking factors:

First, international law and agreements are accompanied by international organisations to create an international system that goes significantly beyond one of just states. The archetypal example of such an organisation is the United Nations, which pools resources for common goals (such as ameliorating climate change), provides for near constant diplomacy between enemies and friends alike and gives all member states a voice in the international community.

Second, the spread of free trade and capitalism through the efforts of powerful liberal states and international organisations like the World Trade Organization, the International Monetary Fund and the World Bank creates an open, market-based, international economic system. This situation is mutually beneficial as a high level of trade between states decreases conflict and makes war less likely, since war would disrupt or cancel the benefits (profits) of trade. States with extensive trade ties are therefore strongly incentivised to maintain peaceful relations. By this calculation, war is not profitable, but detrimental to the state.

The third element of the liberal international order is international norms. Liberal norms favour international cooperation, human rights, democracy and rule of law. When a state takes actions contrary to these norms, they are subject to various types of costs. However, international norms are often contested because of the wide variation in values around the globe. Nevertheless, there are costs for violating liberal norms. The costs can be direct and immediate. For example, the European Union placed an arms sale embargo on China following its violent suppression of pro-democracy protesters in 1989. The embargo continues to this day. The costs can also be less direct, but equally as significant. For example, favourable views of the United States decreased significantly around the world following the 2003 invasion of Iraq because the invasion was undertaken unilaterally (outside established United Nations rules) in a move that was widely deemed illegitimate.

Most liberal scholarship today focuses on how international organisations foster cooperation by helping states overcome the incentive to escape from international agreements. This type of scholarship is commonly referred to as 'neoliberal institutionalism' – often shortened to just 'neoliberalism'. This often causes confusion as neoliberalism is also a term used outside IR theory to describe a widespread economic ideology of deregulation, privatisation, low taxes, austerity (public spending cuts) and free trade. The essence of neoliberalism, when applied within IR, is that states can benefit significantly from cooperation if they trust one another to live up to their agreements. In situations where a state can gain from cheating and escape punishment, defection is likely. However, when a third party (such as an impartial international organisation) is able to monitor the behaviour of signatories to an agreement and provide information to both sides, the incentive to defect decreases and both sides can commit to cooperate. In these cases, all signatories to the agreement can benefit from absolute gains. Absolute gains refer to a general increase in welfare for all parties concerned – everyone benefits to some degree, though not necessarily equally. Liberal theorists argue that states care more about absolute gains than relative gains. Relative gains, which relate closely to realist accounts, describe a situation where a state measures its increase in welfare relative to other states and may shy away from any agreements that make a competitor stronger. By focusing on the more optimistic viewpoint of absolute gains and providing evidence of its existence via international organisations, liberals see a world where states will likely cooperate in any agreement where any increase in prosperity is probable.

Liberal theory and American imperialism

One of the more interesting illustrations of liberalism comes from the foreign policy of the United States during the early twentieth century. During this period, the United States was liberal, but according to the dominant historical narrative, also imperialistic (see Meiser 2015). So, there appears to be a contradiction. If we take a closer look we see that the United States was more restrained than commonly believed, particularly relative to other great powers of that era. One simple measure is the level of colonial territory it accrued compared to other great powers. By 1913, the United States claimed 310,000 square kilometres of colonial territory, compared to 2,360,000 for Belgium, 2,940,000 for Germany and 32,860,000 for the United Kingdom (Bairoch 1993, 83). In fact, the bulk of American colonial holdings was due to the annexation of the Philippines and Puerto Rico, which it inherited after defeating Spain in the Spanish-American War of 1898. The United States exhibited such restraint because, as suggested by liberal theory, its political structure limited expansionism. Examining US–Mexico relations during the early twentieth century helps illustrate the causes of this American restraint.

In the spring of 1914, the United States invaded the Mexican city of Veracruz because of a dispute over the detention of several American sailors in Mexico. However, US–Mexican relations were already troubled because of President Woodrow Wilson's liberal belief that it was the duty of the United States to bring democracy to Mexico, which was a dictatorship. The initial objectives of the American war plan were to occupy Veracruz and neighbouring Tampico and then blockade the east coast of Mexico until American honour was vindicated – or a regime change occurred in Mexico. After American forces landed in Veracruz, senior military leaders and Wilson's top diplomatic advisor in Mexico advocated an escalation of the political objectives to include occupation of Mexico City – there were also vocal proponents who advocated the full occupation of Mexico. Wilson did not actually follow any of the advice he received. Instead, he reduced his war aims, halted his forces at Veracruz and withdrew US forces within a few months. Wilson exercised restraint because of American public opposition, his own personal values, unified Mexican hostility and the military losses incurred in the fighting. International opinion also appears to have influenced Wilson's thinking as anti-Americanism began to sweep through Latin America. As Arthur Link points out, 'Altogether, it was an unhappy time for a President and a people who claimed the moral leadership of the world' (Link 1956, 405).

By 1919, a pro-interventionist coalition developed in the United States built on frustration with President Wilson's prior restraint and new fears over the Mexican Constitution of 1917, which gave the Mexican people ownership of all subsoil resources. This potentially endangered foreign ownership of mines and oilfields in Mexico. Interventionists wanted to turn Mexico into an American protectorate – or at least seize the Mexican oil fields. This coalition moved the country toward intervention while Wilson was distracted by peace negotiations in Europe and then bedridden by a stroke. The path to intervention was blocked only after Wilson recovered sufficiently to regain command of the policy agenda and sever the ties between the interventionists. Wilson had two main reasons for avoiding the more belligerent policy path. First, he saw the Houses of Congress (with the support of some members of the executive branch) attempting to determine the foreign policy of the United States, which Wilson viewed as unconstitutional. In the American system, the president has the authority to conduct foreign policy. His assertion of authority over foreign policy with Mexico was therefore a clear attempt to check the power of Congress in policymaking. Second, Wilson was determined to maintain a policy consistent with the norm of anti-imperialism, but also the norm of self-determination – the process by which a country determines its own statehood and chooses its own form of government. Both of these norms remain bedrocks of liberal theory today.

US relations with Mexico in this case show how institutional and normative domestic structures restrained the use of violent power. These institutional restraints can break down if the political culture of a society does not include a strong dose of liberal norms. For example, anti-statism (a belief that the power of the government should be limited) and anti-imperialism (a belief that conquest of foreign peoples is wrong) are liberal norms. A society infused by liberal norms has an added level of restraint above and beyond the purely institutional limitations on state power. A liberal citizenry will naturally oppose government actions that threaten individual liberty and choose representatives that will act on liberal preferences. The institutional separation of powers in the United States allowed Wilson to block the interventionist efforts of Congress and others. The liberal norm of anti-imperialism restrained American expansion through the mechanisms of public opinion and the personal values of the president of the United States. Institutions and norms worked symbiotically. International opinion put additional pressure on American political leaders due to increasing trade opportunities with Latin American countries throughout the early 1900s. Precisely as liberal theory details, the absolute gains and opportunities offered by trade, together with preferences for self-determination and non-interference, acted as a restraint on US expansionism toward Mexico in this most imperial of periods in world history.

Conclusion

A core argument of liberalism is that concentrations of unaccountable violent power are the fundamental threat to individual liberty and must be restrained. The primary means of restraining power are institutions and norms at both domestic and international level. At the international level institutions and organisations limit the power of states by fostering cooperation and providing a means for imposing costs on states that violate international agreements. Economic institutions are particularly effective at fostering cooperation because of the substantial benefits that can be derived from economic interdependence. Finally, liberal norms add a further limitation on the use of power by shaping our understanding of what types of behaviour are appropriate. Today, it is clear that liberalism is not a 'utopian' theory describing a dream world of peace and happiness as it was once accused of being. It provides a consistent rejoinder to realism, firmly rooted in evidence and a deep theoretical tradition.

3

The English School

YANNIS A. STIVACHTIS

The English school provides the basis for the study of international and world history in terms of the social structures of international orders. Unlike many theories that claim a certain sector of the subject of International Relations, the English school provides a holistic approach to the subject, attempting to see the world as a whole. English school theory is built around establishing distinctions between three key concepts: international system, international society and world society. By doing so it opens up a new space in IR theory and offers a middle ground between the opposing theories of realism and liberalism.

The basics of the English school

The English school is built around three key concepts: *international system*, *international society* and *world society*. Hedley Bull (1977, 9–10) defined the international system as being formed 'when two or more states have sufficient contact between them, and have sufficient impact on one another's decisions to cause them to behave as parts of a whole.' According to this definition, the international system is mainly about power politics among states whose actions are conditioned by the structure of international anarchy. An international society exists when a group of like-minded states 'conceive themselves to be bound by a common set of rules in their relations with one another, and share in the working of common institutions' (Bull 1977, 13). In other words, international society is about the creation and maintenance of shared norms, rules and institutions. Finally, world society is more fundamental than international society because 'the ultimate units of the great society of all mankind are not states ... but individual human beings' (Bull 1977, 21). Thus, world society transcends the state system and takes individuals, non-state actors and ultimately the global population as the focus of global societal identities and arrangements. It is important to note here that in the English school the term 'institution' is different to the term 'organisation'.

According to English school thought, 'institutions' refer to long-term practices among states (such as diplomacy, law and war) rather than to international bureaucratic structures (organisations) that may be established to facilitate state interaction. To refer to international organisations, the English school uses the term 'pseudo-institutions' or 'secondary institutions' to show that the effectiveness of international organisations depends on the function of an international society's primary institutions.

The distinction between an international *system* and an international *society* helps us distinguish the pattern and character of relations among and between certain states and groups of states. For example, historically there was an essential difference between the type of relations among the European states and the type of their relations with the Ottoman Empire. Relations among the European states reflected the existence of a European international *society*, while relations between the European states and the Ottoman Empire reflected the existence of an international *system*. Likewise, the interaction among the European Union's member states reflects the existence of an *international society*, while the interaction of the European Union itself with Turkey (a non-member) describes interaction within a broader *international system*. Despite its usefulness, the distinction between an international system and an international society invited considerable criticism because even in an international system one could observe the existence of some rules and the operation of some institutions. This debate has resulted in the acceptance of the premise that an international system constitutes a weak or 'thin' form of an international society.

Throughout the bulk of history, there was not any single international system or society. Instead, there were several regional international societies, each with its own distinctive rules and institutions. All were built upon elaborate civilisations, including distinctive religions, different systems of governance, different types of law and different conceptions of the world. This, in turn, implied that relations between political entities that were members of different regional international societies could not be conducted on the same moral and legal basis as relations within the same society, because the rules of each individual regional society were culturally particular and exclusive. There was no single agreed body of rules and institutions operating across the boundaries of any two or more regional international societies to speak for a broad international society. Moreover, contacts between regional international societies were much more limited than contacts within them. Thus, the emergence of a truly universal international society would not be possible unless one of the regional international societies could expand itself to the degree that it could merge all the others into a single universal society organised around a common body of rules and values.

During the seventeenth and eighteenth centuries, international society came to be regarded as a privileged association of European and 'civilised' states, which had visible expression in certain institutions such as international law, diplomacy and the balance of power. There was a sense that European powers were bound by a code of conduct in their dealings with one another and that this code did not apply in their dealings with other societies. Nineteenth-century international lawyers perpetuated the cultural duality between Europeans and non-Europeans and between 'civilised' and 'non-civilised' peoples. The distinction between 'civilised' and 'barbarous' humanity meant that states belonging to either category were accorded different stages of legal recognition. As the European international society spread over the world, many non-European states sought to join international society. Thus, the European states needed to define the conditions under which non-European political entities would be admitted. The result was the establishment of a standard of 'civilisation', which reflected the norms of the liberal European civilisation.

The standard of civilisation included such elements as the guarantee of basic human rights and the maintenance of a domestic legal system guaranteeing justice for all. Thus, by definition, countries unwilling or unable to guarantee such rights could not be considered 'civilised'. Consequently, non-European candidate states were judged not only by how they conducted their foreign relations but also by how they governed themselves. The process also led to the creation of hierarchical relations between two new categories of states: the 'civilisers' and the 'civilisees'. Or to put it another way, the 'teachers' and the 'pupils'.

A new international society emerged following the end of the First World War (1914–1918), watermarked by the establishment of the League of Nations in 1920. The latter's design for a new global international society incorporated almost all the rules and practices that had developed in the European international society, including its international law and diplomacy, as well as its basic assumptions about sovereignty and the judicial equality of states recognised as independent members of the society. The impetus for the League came not from Europe, but from an American president, Woodrow Wilson – signifying a change in the nature of the international order. The outbreak of the Second World War in 1939 interrupted the functioning of the League and consequently led to the destruction of that particular international society. The establishment of the United Nations (UN) in 1945 constituted the expression of yet another new international society. In fact, many principles and structures found in the League were replicated by the United Nations. Meanwhile, the standard of 'civilisation' was insulting to representatives of non-European civilisations since the privileged legal status which European states claimed for themselves meant not only the division of the world between 'civilised' and 'non-civilised' states but also the maintenance of a hierarchical relationship among states. Consequently, non-European states and colonised communities began campaigning against the 'standard of civilisation', which was eventually abolished when the decolonisation process commenced – heralding the end of the age of empire and imperialism. The emergence of the bipolar world of the Cold War (1947–1991), when two superpowers divided the world into their respective orbits, led to the division of the relatively 'thin' new global international society into two sub-global 'thicker' international societies: one associated with the United States and one with the Soviet Union. The end of the Cold War in 1991 meant two things: first, the division of the global international society ceased to exist; and second, a set of regional international societies with different degrees of 'thickness' gradually emerged within the confines of the 'thinner' global international society.

A key debate within the English school revolves around pluralism and solidarism. Pluralism refers to international societies with a relatively low degree of shared norms, rules and institutions. Solidarism refers to types of international society with a relatively high degree of shared norms, rules and institutions. The pluralist/solidarist debate is basically about how international society relates to world society or, in other words, to people. The main question has been how to reduce the tension between the needs and imperatives of states and the needs and imperatives of humankind. These are regularly in conflict both in real world situations and in the theory. Most English school scholars operate within this debate, taking the tension between the imperatives of order and justice as the core problem to be addressed.

Important to the pluralist/solidarist debate are questions about whether international law should include natural law or positive law. *Natural law* is a philosophy that advocates that certain rights or values are inherent by virtue of human nature and can be universally understood through human reason. In other words, natural law refers to a body of unchanging moral principles regarded as a basis for all human conduct. Positive law, on the other hand, refers to human-made laws of a given community, society or state. This debate manifests most acutely between states' claims to sovereignty (via pluralism) on the one hand and the idea that universal rights are vested in people (via solidarism) on the other. A quick example to demonstrate this would be to use the case of Syria. A pluralist reading would state that despite terrible atrocities since 2011 as the state has collapsed in a brutal civil war, Syria is a sovereign country and responsible for its own territory and people. A solidarist position would stress the overriding obligation to protect human life and intervene in Syria's civil war. Both positions would suggest a very different type of international society. Pluralism and solidarism, while seemingly opposites, are the framing principles for a debate about the limits and possibilities of international society. This debate is mostly about how best to reconcile the desires and needs of both people and states. In this sense, the English school is an essential tool within IR theory that tries to find a working balance between how power, interests and standards of justice and responsibility operate in international society.

The English school and the European Union

Following the end of the Second World War in 1945, six European states formed a regional international system in the sense that they had 'sufficient contact between them, and had sufficient impact on one another's decisions to cause them to behave as parts of a whole' (Bull 1977, 9–10). Applying Bull's definition of international society, relatively soon an international society was formed in the sense that 'they conceive themselves to be bound by a common set of rules in their relations with one another, and share in the working of common institutions' (Bull 1977, 13). In other words, these European states that today are associated with the European Union (EU) created a set of rules and institutions to govern and manage their affairs. As time progressed, the integration process gained strength, breadth and depth, resulting in the creation of supranational institutions (legal powers existing beyond the state), law and policies. This, in turn, led, among other things, to the creation of an EU world society that underpins the EU international society. At the same time, EU law and policies seek to regulate the relations between the Union and, on the one hand, its member states and, on the other, its people. In this way, the tension between the needs and imperatives of states and the needs and imperatives of people, as well as the tension between the imperatives of order and justice, which constitute the core of the pluralist/solidarist debate, are addressed.

The process of the EU enlargement as it went from six members in 1951 to 28 in 2013 is not very different from the process of the historical expansion of European international society. As in the nineteenth and early twentieth centuries, EU member states had to define the conditions under which they would admit candidate states. As a result, European states that aspire to EU membership need to meet specific political and economic criteria. Like the historical standard of 'civilisation', the EU's membership conditions are an expression of the assumptions used to distinguish those that belong to the expanding Union from those that do not. Those that fulfil the political and economic conditions set by the EU states will be brought inside while those that do not conform will be left outside. Like the non-European states before, EU candidate states had to learn to adjust themselves to new realities, sometimes at significant cost to their own societies.

The EU's membership criteria include both economic and political conditions. Because the EU started as an economic organisation, the definition of the economic conditions that prospective members must meet was in place from the beginning. On the other hand, the formulation of political conditions has undergone considerable evolution. At its Copenhagen Summit in June 1993, EU norms and values were clarified under the following criteria:

1. Membership requires that the candidate country has achieved stability of institutions guaranteeing democracy, the rule of law, human rights, and respect for the protection of minorities.

2. Membership requires the existence of a functioning market economy as well as the capacity to cope with competitive pressure and market forces within the Union.

3. Membership presupposes the candidate's ability to take on the obligations of membership including adherence to the aims of political, economic and monetary union.

The EU's potential for impacting on candidate states varies between two broad stages: first, pre-negotiations (when the Copenhagen criteria must be satisfied before negotiations commence); and second, actual negotiations (when political conditions are monitored regularly). During the first phase, negotiations may be blocked by a country's failure to satisfy the political conditions, while during the second phase, negotiations may be interrupted or terminated if a negotiating country reverses its fulfilment of the political conditions or violates any of them. Here the case of Turkey comes to mind, considering its authoritarian power shifts and troubled human rights record – which may explain why its path to membership has gone unfulfilled since it first applied to join in 1987.

The process of EU enlargement, steadily growing to cover the bulk of the European continent, demonstrates how a 'thick' regional international society expands outwards, gradually transforming the much broader international system in which it is embedded into an international society. But, as noted earlier, the international system itself represents a 'thin' form of an inter-national society.

However, the expansion process does not end with the entry of candidate states into the European Union. In fact, elements of order present in the EU and which are associated with international society and world society are exported beyond the Union's boundaries in three additional ways. First, states located around the EU's borders are encouraged to adopt norms and practices compatible with those of the European Union. Second, to access development assistance or aid, states must fulfil certain political and economic conditions that reflect EU norms and values. Third, asking trading partners to adhere to certain norms, rules and practices have become EU conditions that have shaped the Union's trade policy and its relations with external states.

If the study of the EU enlargement is important to understand how regional international societies expand outwards, thereby slowly transforming the much broader international system in which they are embedded into an international society, the investigation of what happens to them if they contract is equally important. For example, what would happen to the EU regional international society as a result of 'Brexit' (the United Kingdom leaving the European Union) and the possibility that other states may also leave? There are two possibilities. First, if core members of a regional international society depart, then this society may be gradually transformed into a 'thinner' international society, which is equivalent to an international system. Second, the regional international society may continue to exist, but the states that leave this society would move into the broader international system in which the regional international society is embedded.

For example, despite Brexit, the EU regional international society will continue to exist but the United Kingdom would move into the broader international system in which the EU regional international society is embedded. But if other EU member states follow the same path, then the EU regional international society will be gradually transformed into a 'thinner' international society, which is equivalent to an international system. Unless the EU member states come together to commonly confront its challenges (of which Brexit is only one), we may gradually see a decrease in the EU's 'thickness', which implies a movement from the world society end of the spectrum to the international system end of the spectrum.

Conclusion

Two important debates have taken place within the English school. First, whether the distinction between an international system and an international society is valid and, if yes, then where does the boundary line between the two forms of international order lie. The second turns on pluralist versus solidarist understandings and the relationship between international society and world society. The first debate has resulted in the acceptance of the premise that an international system constitutes a weak/thin form of an international society. Although the pluralist/solidarist debate is still ongoing, one should recognise that certain changes in international society (e.g. a shift from a world of perpetual war pre-1945 to a world of relative peace post-1945) are accompanied by some other important developments in world society. For example, there has been a growing demand for human rights as people increasingly understand that they are embedded in a single global economy and a single global environment. At the same time, technology and social media enable widely shared experiences. These developments have led to an increased interplay between international society and world society that has the potential of stabilising international society by embedding ideas not just in the minds of political and economic elites but also in the minds of ordinary citizens.

4

Constructivism

SARINA THEYS

Constructivism's arrival in IR is often associated with the end of the Cold War, an event that the traditional theories such as realism and liberalism failed to account for. This failure can be linked to some of their core tenets, such as the conviction that states are self-interested actors who compete for power and the unequal power distribution among states which defines the balance of power between them. By having a dominant focus on the state, traditional theories have not opened much space to observe the agency of individuals. After all, it was the actions of ordinary people that ensured the end of the Cold War, not those of states or international organisations. Constructivism accounts for this issue by arguing that the social world is of our making (Onuf 1989). Actors (usually powerful ones, like leaders and influential citizens) continually shape – and sometimes reshape – the very nature of international relations through their actions and interactions.

The basics of constructivism

Constructivism sees the world, and what we can know about the world, as socially constructed. This view refers to the nature of reality and the nature of knowledge that are also called ontology and epistemology in research language. Alexander Wendt (1995) offers an excellent example that illustrates the social construction of reality when he explains that 500 British nuclear weapons are less threatening to the United States than five North Korean nuclear weapons. These identifications are not caused by the nuclear weapons (the *material structure*) but rather by the meaning given to the material structure (the *ideational structure*). It is important to understand that the social relationship between the United States and Britain and the United States and North Korea is perceived in a similar way by these states, as this shared understanding (or intersubjectivity) forms the basis of their interactions. The example also shows that nuclear weapons by themselves do not have any meaning unless we understand the social context. It further demonstrates that constructivists go beyond the material reality by including the effect of ideas and beliefs on world politics. This also entails that reality is always under construction, which opens the prospect for change. In other words, meanings are not fixed but can change over time depending on the ideas and beliefs that actors hold.

Constructivists argue that agency and structure are mutually constituted, which implies that structures influence agency and that agency influences structures. Agency can be understood as the ability of someone to act, whereas structure refers to the international system that consists of material and ideational elements. Returning to Wendt's example discussed above, this means that the social relation of enmity between the United States and North Korea represents the intersubjective structure (that is, the shared ideas and beliefs among both states), whereas the United States and North Korea are the actors who have the capacity (that is, agency) to change or reinforce the existing structure or social relationship of enmity. This change or reinforcement ultimately depends on the beliefs and ideas held by both states. If these beliefs and ideas change, the social relationship can change to one of friendship. This stance differs considerably from that of realists, who argue that the anarchic structure of the international system determines the behaviour of states. Constructivists, on the other hand, argue that 'anarchy is what states make of it' (Wendt 1992). This means that anarchy can be interpreted in different ways depending on the meaning that actors assign to it.

Another central issue to constructivism is identities and interests. Constructivists argue that states can have multiple identities that are socially constructed through interaction with other actors. Identities are representations of an actor's understanding of who they are, which in turn signals their interests. They are important to constructivists as they argue that identities constitute interests and actions. For example, the identity of a small state implies a set of interests that are different from those implied by the identity of a large state. The small state is arguably more focused on its survival, whereas the large state is concerned with dominating global political, economic and military affairs. It should be noted, though, that the actions of a state should be aligned with its identity. A state can thus not act contrary to its identity because this will call into question the validity of the identity, including its preferences. This issue might explain why Germany, despite being a great power with a leading global economy, did not become a military power in the second half of the twentieth century. Following the atrocities of Adolf Hitler's Nazi regime during the Second World War, German political identity shifted from one of militarism to pacifism due to unique historical circumstances.

Social norms are also central to constructivism. These are generally defined as 'a standard of appropriate behaviour for actors with a given identity' (Katzenstein 1996, 5). States that conform to a certain identity are expected to comply with the norms that are associated with that identity. This idea comes with an expectation that some kinds of behaviour and action are more acceptable than others. This process is also known as 'the logic of app-ropriateness', where actors behave in certain ways because they believe that this behaviour is appropriate (March and Olsen 1998, 951–952). To better understand norms, we can identify three types: regulative norms, constitutive norms and prescriptive norms. *Regulative norms* order and constrain behaviour; *constitutive norms* create new actors, interests or categories of action; and *prescriptive norms* prescribe certain norms, meaning there are no bad norms from the perspective of those who promote them (Finnemore and Sikkink 1998). It is also important to note that norms go through a 'lifecycle of norms' before they can get accepted. A norm only becomes an expected behaviour when a critical mass of relevant state actors adopt it and internalise it in their own practices. For example, constructivists would argue that the bulk of states have come together to develop climate change mitigation policies because it is the right thing to do for the survival of humanity. This has, over decades of diplomacy and advocacy, become an appropriate behaviour that the bulk of citizens expect their leaders to adhere to. Liberals, on the other hand, might reject the notion of climate change politics in favour of continued economic growth and pursuing innovative scientific solutions, while realists might reject it due to the damage that climate policies may do to shorter-term national interests.

Although all constructivists share the above-mentioned views and concepts, there is considerable variety within constructivism. Conventional constru-ctivists ask 'what'-type questions – such as *what causes an actor to act*. They believe that it is possible to explain the world in causal terms and are interested in discovering the relationships between actors, social norms, interests and identities. Conventional constructivists assume, for instance, that actors act according to their identity and that it is possible to predict when this identity becomes visible or not. When an identity is seen to be under-going changes, conventional constructivists investigate what factors caused which aspects of a state's identity to change. Critical constructivists, on the other hand, ask 'how'-type questions such as *how do actors come to believe in a certain identity*. Contrary to conventional constructivists, they are not interested in the effect that this identity has. Instead, critical constructivists want to reconstruct an identity – that is, find out what are its component parts – which they believe are created through written or spoken communication among and between peoples. Language plays a key role for critical cons-tructivists because it constructs, and has the ability to change, social reality.

Most constructivists, however, position themselves between these two more extreme ends of the spectrum.

Constructivism and Bhutan's national interests

Bhutan is a Buddhist kingdom located in the Himalayas. The material structural conditions are reflected in its population of approximately 745,000, a territory that amounts to 38,394 square kilometres, a weak economy and a very small military. On top of this, Bhutan shares a national border with the two major powers in Asia: China in the north and India in the south. Bhutan's location is geographically sensitive as the country serves as a buffer state between these major powers, which perceive each other as rivals rather than friends. In addition to this, the Chinese leadership claimed, after it annexed Tibet in the 1950s, that Bhutan's territory was also part of its mainland. To date there remains an ongoing border dispute between Bhutan and China and there have been reports that the Chinese army has made several incursions into Bhutan. Likewise, India has had a hand in Bhutan's foreign policy. Article 2 of the India-Bhutan Friendship Treaty (1949) notes that 'Bhutan agrees to be guided by the advice of India in regard to its external relations.' Although this Article was revised in 2007, commentators have reported that India still holds a degree of influence over Bhutan.

From a realist perspective, one would argue that Bhutan is in an unfavourable position as it is hindered by its geographical location and cannot compete for power with its neighbours. The preservation of its national sovereignty would likely depend on the outcome of the greater competition between China and India. A constructivist view, on the other hand, would argue that these structural conditions do not necessarily constrain Bhutan's ability to pursue its national interests since they are not the only conditions that influence state behaviour: the *meaning* given to these structural conditions also matters. For example, when Tibet was annexed by China, Bhutan felt threatened. As a result, it closed its border in the north and turned to India, its neighbour in the south. From that moment onward, Bhutan perceived China as a potential threat and India as a friend. To date, Bhutan and India perceive each other as friends whereas Bhutan has no official relations with China. These social relationships represent the ideational structure that originated from the meaning given to the material structure. It is important to note, however, that the social relationships are subject to change depending on the ideas, beliefs and actions of Bhutan, India and China. For example, an agreement on the border dispute between China and Bhutan could change how both countries perceive each other. This change might lead to the establishment of an official relationship, the nature of which is friendship rather than enmity. A constructivist is well placed to detect and understand these changes since their object of enquiry focuses on the social relationships between states.

Bhutan has also developed a distinctive national identity that differentiates it from its larger neighbours. This identity projects Bhutan as 'the last surviving independent Mahayana Buddhist Kingdom in the world' (Bhutan Vision 2020, 24–25). The usage of the word 'independent' refers directly to Bhutan's national interest – the preservation of its national sovereignty. Bhutan's national identity is socially constructed through a *Bhutanisation* process that started in the 1980s, when the fourth king of Bhutan introduced the 'One Nation, One People' policy. This policy demanded the observance of a code of conduct known as *Driglam Namzhag*. This code of conduct is built upon strict observance of vows – such as strong kinship loyalty, respect for one's parents, elders and superiors, and mutual cooperation between rulers and ruled. It also reinforced the rules for wearing a national dress – the *gho* for men and the *kira* for women. In addition to this, Dzongkha was selected as the national language of Bhutan. The Driglam Namzhag can be thought of as a regulative norm because the aim of the policy is to direct and constrain behaviour. For example, although Bhutan's national identity suggests that the Bhutanese comprise one homogeneous group, Bhutan is actually a multi-ethnic, multi-religious and multi-lingual country. There are three main ethnic groups: the Ngalongs, the Sharchhops and the Lhotshampas, who are of Nepali descent. Of these, the Ngalongs and the Sharchhops are Buddhists, while the Lhotshampas are mostly Hindus who speak the Nepali language. The policy had severe consequences for the Lhotshampas as Nepali was no longer taught in schools and people who could not prove residence in Bhutan prior to 1958 were classified as non-nationals. Consequently, thousands of Lhotshampas were expelled from Bhutan in the 1990s. Thus, the code of conduct is used by the Bhutanese authorities to create cultural unity and to stimulate citizens to reflect upon their cultural distinctiveness, which is paramount in creating a national identity.

As mentioned earlier in the chapter, a norm needs to go through a lifecycle before it becomes established. In the case of Bhutan, we can witness the first phase, *norm emergence*, in the creation of the Driglam Namzhag by the Bhutanese authorities. The second phase, *norm acceptance*, required Bhutanese citizens to accept the Driglam Namzhag, including the national dress and Dzongkha as the national language. Once this acceptance occurred, *norm internalisation* occurs. The completion of this process entails that the behaviour of the Bhutanese citizens is circumscribed by these norms and practices. This circumscription also shows the constitutive nature of the Driglam Namzhag, which created new actors – that is, Bhutanese citizens who act and behave according to specific rules. We can see, for instance, that these norms and practices are regulated to date. For example, Bhutanese citizens are obliged to wear the national dress during national events and when they attend school or work. This regulation is, as explained earlier, important as the behaviour of a state and its citizens should comply with the norms that are associated with Bhutan's national identity. The regulation also signifies that these norms are perceived as something good by the Bhutanese authorities, which underlines the prescriptive nature of norms.

Members of the Bhutanese elite have also created a second identity, which projects Bhutan as a leader in advancing a holistic and sustainable development paradigm. This identity is based on Bhutan's development philosophy, Gross National Happiness (GNH), which criticises the well-known Gross Domestic Product (GDP) approach for being solely focused on the economy of a state. Instead, GNH promotes a balance between material wellbeing and the spiritual needs of the mind. It is implemented and embedded in Bhutan's political and educational systems. Members of the Bhutanese elite have predominantly used the United Nations as a platform to promote the idea internationally. Subsequently, the United Nations adopted Resolution 65/309, which states that the pursuit of happiness is a fundamental goal and that the gross domestic product indicator was not designed to, and does not adequately reflect, the wellbeing of people. Projecting their country as the last surviving independent Mahayana Buddhist kingdom in the world and as a leader in advancing a holistic and sustainable development paradigm enables Bhutanese authorities to signal their country's status as an independent sovereign state. It also allows Bhutan to increase its international visibility, which is advantageous when tensions run high with and among its neighbours.

Conclusion

Constructivism is often said to simply state the obvious – that actions, interactions and perceptions shape reality. Indeed, that idea is the source of the name of this theory family. Our thoughts and actions literally *construct* international relations. Yet, this seemingly simple idea, when applied theoretically, has significant implications for how we can understand the world. The discipline of International Relations benefits from constructivism as it addresses issues and concepts that are neglected by mainstream theories – especially realism. Doing so, constructivists offer alternative explanations and insights for events occurring in the social world. They show, for instance, that it is not only the distribution of material power, wealth and geographical conditions that can explain state behaviour but also ideas, identities and norms. Furthermore, their focus on ideational factors shows that reality is not fixed, but rather subject to change.

5

Marxism

MAÏA PAL

Marxism is both a critical approach that wants to always question the mainstream policy-driven approaches to IR theory and a classical approach via the philosophical and sociological tradition of its namesake, the philosopher Karl Marx (1818–1883). In fact, Marxism is the only theoretical perspective in IR that is named after a person. Of the range of great thinkers available to us, Marx may not automatically qualify as being the most 'internationalist'. In fact, most of Marx's (and his sometimes co-author Friedrich Engels') work was not primarily concerned with the formation of states or even the interactions between them. What connected their interests to IR was the industrial revolution, as this event was ultimately what Marx was witnessing and trying to understand. He, with Engels, developed a revolutionary approach and outlined a set of concepts that transcended national differences while also providing practical advice on how to build a transnational movement of people. Workers from factories across the world – the *proletariat* – were to organise themselves into a politically revolutionary movement to counter the exploitative and unequal effects of capitalism, which were accelerated and expanded by the industrial revolution. This vision of a potential link between the bulk of humanity as a global proletariat is where, and how, Marxism enters IR from a different vantage point to other theories.

The basics of Marxism

Marxist concepts are all connected by the common goal to contribute to what they perceive as the greater good of humankind and its environment. To borrow the words of Adrienne Rich (2002, 65), theory is

> the seeing of patterns, showing the forest as well as the trees
> – theory can be a dew that rises from the earth and collects in

> the rain cloud and returns to earth over and over. But if it
> doesn't smell of the earth, it isn't good for the earth.

In other words, Marxists must remain informed and reflective of the basic and most common aspects of societies and their environment. This also means that if the industrial revolution (and capitalism in general) smells of burning coal, overcrowded factories and petrol fumes, the smells of the next revolution should be less deadly, less polluting and more protective of the earth. To understand Marxism, we need to grasp the basic elements of Marx's innovations regarding the origins and functioning of capitalism. In addition, we must understand that those origins and functioning can simultaneously happen at the domestic and international level. Combining these tasks leads to arguably the most important contribution Marxism offers to IR: that the capitalist mode of production and the modern sovereign states system (that emerged roughly at the same time) are not natural or inevitable events. They are interdependent products of particular historical conditions and social relations. The work of Marxists is to map and retrace those conditions and social relations and to figure out how the capitalist mode of production and the sovereign states system emerged – as two sides of the same coin, as different coins or maybe as different currencies. Debates on the degree of interdependence between these two major historical phenomena may be ongoing, but Marxism's achievement in IR has been to stop us from thinking about them separately. Marxism also advises that concepts are not just meant to help us understand the world – they should also help us change it.

To explain Marxism in IR, we need to start with Marx's main theory for the development of capitalism: historical materialism. Most simply, historical materialism asserts that human beings – including their relations with each other and their environment – are determined by the material conditions in which they can survive and reproduce. Therefore, Marxism asserts that material conditions can be changed by the actions of human beings as well as by events – think of climate change for example, which depends on physical phenomena as well as human behaviour. In other words, these material conditions are historical, they change over space and time. But they are also always dependent on – and often hampered by – the processes and ideas that preceded them, as the past weighs on the present. A Marxist would stress that IR is not just about states' foreign policy or the behaviour of politicians, but more about survival (or more broadly, life), reproduction, technologies and labour. If this is correct then the separation between the political and economic, or public and private, is problematic because those categories hide the ways in which states and foreign policies are determined by the social relations and structures of the global economy – such as multinational corporations or international financial institutions. Put differently, Marxism fundamentally questions what 'the international' is in IR. Whether it is anarchy for realists or international society for the English school, Marxists argue that such concepts are problematic because they make us believe in illusions or myths about the world. For example, the concept of anarchy creates the mirage that states are autonomous agents whose rational behaviour can be predicted. However, this ignores the endurance of regional inequalities and the structural and historical links between states, violence and the key actors of the global political economy.

The first application of Marxist ideas to explain international processes was by communists and revolutionaries of the early twentieth century such as Rosa Luxemburg, Rudolf Hilferding and Vladimir Lenin. These authors developed what we now call the classical theories of imperialism to understand how capitalism expanded and adapted to a world of inter-imperial rivalry leading to the First World War and the slow disintegration of the European empires.

In 1974, Immanuel Wallerstein developed 'world systems theory' to incorporate the changes of the late twentieth century and counter the way traditional approaches tended to understand imperialism as a state-led process. Wallerstein's approach used different units of analysis and took a much longer-term view of the history of states and their interactions. He distinguished three groups of states or regions: the core, the semi-periphery and the periphery. The aim was to understand how states have developed since the sixteenth century in relation to each other, thereby creating relations of dependency between different groups of states depending on the specific types of economies and industries they specialised in. Therefore, these relations of dependency and groups required that we understand the world through broader units than states. These units – or world systems – helped to address the dilemma of why states all became capitalist, albeit in very unequal and different ways. The core group of states (e.g. in Western Europe and North America) refers to democratic governments providing high wages and encouraging high levels of investment and welfare services. The semi-periphery states (e.g. in Latin America) are authoritarian governments that provide low wages and poor welfare services for their citizens. Periphery states (e.g. sub-Saharan and Central Africa, South Asia) refer to non-democratic governments where workers can mostly expect wages below subsistence levels and where there are no welfare services.

The core is able to produce high-profit consumption goods for itself as well as for the semi-periphery and periphery markets because the periphery provides the cheap labour and raw materials to the core and semi-periphery necessary to make these high-profit consumption goods. In other words, although historically some states have changed their group (e.g. from periphery to semi-periphery), capitalism always needs a peripheral region that provides the means for the core to sustain a high level of consumption and security. Thus, relations of dependency and inequality are essential to capitalism and cannot be significantly reduced.

Another influential update of the classical theories of imperialism is the neo-Gramscian strand of Marxism. Antonio Gramsci's (1891–1937) concept of hegemony is thought by some to be more useful today than the concept of imperialism. It emphasises two things. First, the domination of some groups of individuals (or groups of states) over other groups also depends on ideological factors. In other words, capitalism is experienced in different ways historically and across the globe because people understand it – and therefore agree to or resist it – in different ways. Second, the relations of dependency and types of groups (or units) used to understand those relations are more varied and fluid than world systems theory. Therefore, capitalism dominates our social relations because it is reproduced through coercive *and* consensual means. The concept was used to explain why educated and organised workers in Western Europe did not 'unite' to 'lose their chains', as Marx and Engels had predicted. A neo-Gramscian concept of hegemony focuses on the consensual ways in which transnational classes, organisations and international law reproduce capitalism and its inequalities. The transnational capitalist class – dominated by great powers – forms a 'global civil society' that universalises liberal ideals rather than imposing itself through more coercive processes of classical imperialism and colonisation, as was the case in earlier times.

For example, Singapore, Hong-Kong, South Korea and Taiwan were known as the Four Asian Tigers because of their rapid industrialisation and high growth rates from the 1960s to the 1990s. In these countries, a strong ruling elite consented to a specific type of financial economy – often called a 'neoliberal' model – which also took hold across the world to varying degrees as other states sought to emulate this 'success'. However, vast inequalities and human rights violations are increasing across and within many societies despite the dominance of neoliberalism globally. This shows that although neoliberal hegemony is far from producing the success it originally projected, this *perceived* success remains one of the main drivers of capitalism because it convinces people to consent to capitalism without the threat of force.

A more recent trend of Marxism in IR – historical sociology – returns to some of the more classical problems of IR. Specifically, it looks at the development of the modern state system in relation to the transition(s) to capitalism and to the different moments of colonial and imperial expansion. It looks more closely at what happened inside Europe but also beyond Europe. More specifically, it contests the birth of the sovereign states system following the treaties of Westphalia in 1648 and instead focuses on more socio-economic processes in the nineteenth century to define key shifts in modern international relations. This underlines how scholars are taking history beyond Europe in order to address the Eurocentric assumptions found in Marxism and in the wider discipline of IR itself.

In sum, Marxism is characterised by interdependence. The Marxist term for this is *dialectics*, which underpins the way in which all the previous concepts explored in this chapter relate to each other. For Marxism, all concepts reflect social relations, but categories take on a life of their own and often hide those social relations. It is easy to overcomplicate or abuse this concept. However, it is a crucial starting point for understanding the world as a whole, rather than just its individual parts, since 'dialectics is a way of thinking that brings into focus the full range of changes and interactions that occur in the world' (Ollman 2003, 12).

Marxism, migrants and borders

A Marxist IR approach to migration shows the importance of historical materialism as an approach to IR. First, Marxists are critical of the fixed aspect of borders because they create relations of dependency and inequality between peoples by restricting and controlling their access to resources and labour. Some Marxists argue that we need a global concept of citizenship to counter how states exclude non-citizens from benefits and access to labour and resources. After all, from a Marxist point of view, peoples of all nations are united in their oppression by capitalism and the modern state system that separates them and sets them against each other, so people should be freed (or emancipated) from this status. Consequently, Marxists see borders as fixtures that unfairly determine relations of dependency and inequality – or in other words, who has the right to what. Second, we need to think of who decides who is a migrant and what that category entails. For example, being a migrant who is fleeing a country because of persecution is a necessary condition according to international law for applying for asylum and becoming a refugee in a host state. Most states have signed the 1951 Refugee Convention and have agreed to this definition. Hence, the reality of being this particular type of migrant is dependent on a specific treaty and the will of states to consent to it. In other words, the category of persecuted migrant or refugee is relative – it is not real in the sense that the colour of your eyes is real and cannot be decided differently by someone else.

People who flee from poverty related to conflict, climate change, or lack of jobs are often designated as economic migrants. Their status does not depend on a definition as clear as that of a refugee, and it also does not lead to the same rights and opportunities. Many people move towards Europe because it offers more economic opportunities and a relatively safer political environment. However, decisions at the European and state level are increasingly resulting in the strengthening (or closing) of borders, because some feel that economic migration is not a sufficient reason to freely admit a person. In contrast, being an economic migrant who has a particular skill needed by the host country *is* considered legitimate. In other words, the 'reality' of being a 'good' economic migrant – who is allowed to move across countries – depends on factors that are often independent of the person migrating.

Marxism provides us with an original angle that makes us reconsider migration and shows why closing borders is a sociologically and politically blind policy in relation to the system we all live in. In effect, capitalism started a simultaneous process of territorial bordering and of social change through wage-labour. Mainstream IR separates those processes historically and theoretically by taking the separation between the domestic and international as fixed and real. Marxism argues that this leads to obscuring the social relations and processes linking movements of people and the creation of borders. In other words, dissociating the domestic and international levels leads to thinking that being a migrant is the reserve of certain people rather than a condition we are all subjected to. Crucially, it justifies treating migrants as second-class people and therefore leads to further racial and social inequalities.

Movement of peoples occurred long before capitalism, but capitalism shapes those movements in conjunction with the creation of borders and economic productivity. The process of enclosure at the beginning of capitalism led to people moving away from the land on which they hunted, gathered and grew food. The process involved landowners closing off or fencing common land so as to graze sheep and develop more intensive methods of agriculture. This gradually transformed social relations – the ways in which people could survive and reproduce. Without land to survive on, people had to start selling their ability to work – what Marxists call labour power – and often had to work far from their homes. Although people move for a variety of reasons, one that is particularly familiar is the necessity to move to sell our labour. This can involve transferring from the countryside to an urban centre within a state or from one state to another. In other words, it is the same imperative to work that makes this move happen, whether one crosses an international border or not. In a capitalist system, it is hard to survive without working and working implies moving or being prepared to move. In other words, we are all in theory migrants. Acknowledging this means that closing borders, which involves fixing peoples' status as 'good' or 'bad' economic migrants, is based on two illusions revealed by Marxism and should therefore be questioned and reconsidered. The first is the distinction between domestic and international. Capitalism is an expanding international system and allows domestic borders only in so far as it can transcend them economically. The second illusion is the distinction between categories of people as real and fixed. Capitalism allows the elite to transcend borders economically but also allows the potential to close them politically. Thus, it allows certain people (the most wealthy) to decide that others (the least wealthy) cannot try and change their situations.

Conclusion

The role of theories and knowledge more generally is to reveal what is real and what is an illusion. Historical materialism – the theory that drives Marxism – tries to apply this advice by grounding the understanding of international relations in the ways in which people have transformed the land, produced things on it and are ultimately dependent on its resources for shaping political institutions such as the state and international organisations. Marxism has made several inroads in the development of the discipline of IR by being intrinsically concerned with the ways in which people – and groups – interact and produce things across borders, as well as how they organise themselves through institutions to manage and contest the production and distribution of things across the world. More specifically, it argues that the construction of modern borders is determined by, or linked in various ways to, the development of capitalism. Therefore, it makes us question the natural or inevitable character we tend to ascribe to our economic and political systems. In other words, if a system is not as real and fixed as we first thought, because it has a particular and relatively short history in the broader course of humanity, then it becomes much easier for us to imagine the various ways it is challenged and how it could be transformed to a system that, Marxists hope, will better redistribute the wealth of the world. Marx himself wrote that philosophy is often too concerned with interpreting the world, when the real point is to change it. Marxism as a theory of IR has certainly answered that call and, regardless of variations within the theory family, to be a Marxist always means to challenge one's ideas about the world.

6

Critical Theory

MARCOS FARIAS FERREIRA

Critical theory incorporates a wide range of approaches all focused on the idea of freeing people from the modern state and economic system – a concept known to critical theorists as emancipation. The idea originates from the work of authors such as Immanuel Kant and Karl Marx who, in the eighteenth and nineteenth centuries, advanced different revolutionary ideas of how the world could be reordered and transformed. Both Kant and Marx held a strong attachment to the Enlightenment theme of universalism – the view that there are social and political principles that are apparent to all people, everywhere. In the modern era, both authors became foundational figures for theorists seeking to replace the modern state system by promoting more just global political arrangements such as a federation of free states living in perpetual peace (Kant) or communism as a global social and economic system to replace the unequal capitalist order (Marx). Critical theory sets out to critique repressive social practices and institutions in today's world and advance emancipation by supporting ideas and practices that meet the universalist principles of justice. This kind of critique has a transformative dimension in the sense that it aims at changing national societies, inter-national relations and the emerging global society, starting from alternative ideas and practices lingering in the background of the historical process.

The basics of critical theory

Although critical theory reworks and, in some ways, supersedes Kantian and Marxian themes, both authors remain at the base of the theory's lineage. Through critical philosophy, Kant discussed the conditions in which we make claims about the world and asserted that the increasing interconnectedness of his time opened the door for more cosmopolitan (i.e. supranational) political communities. Marx's critical mode of inquiry was grounded on the will to understand social developments in industrialised societies, including the contradictions inherent in capitalism that would lead to its collapse, the suppression of labour exploitation and the setting up of a more just system of global social relations. This way, the writings of Kant and Marx converge to demonstrate that what happens at the level of international relations is crucial to the achievement of human emancipation and global freedom. Conse-quently, the tracing of tangible social and political possibilities or change (those stemming from within existing practices and institutions) became a defining feature of the strand of critical thought entering IR via authors reworking Marxian and Kantian themes during the twentieth century.

Of course, neither Marx nor Kant were IR theorists in the contemporary sense. Both were philosophers. We must therefore identify two more recent sources for how critical theory developed within the modern discipline of IR. The first is Antonio Gramsci and his influence over Robert Cox and the paradigm of *production* (economic patterns involved in the production of goods and the social and political relationships they entail). The second is the Frankfurt school – Jürgen Habermas in particular – and the influence of Habermas over Andrew Linklater and the paradigm of *communication* (patterns of rationality involved in human communication and the ethical principles they entail). There are two themes uniting these approaches that show the connective glue within the critical theorist family. First, they both use eman-cipation as a principle to critique, or assess, society and the global political order. Second, they both detect the potential for emancipation developing within the historical process, but consider that it may not be inevitable. The paradigms of redistribution and recognition relate to what Nancy Fraser (1995) has called the two main axes of contemporary political struggle. While redistribution struggles refer directly to the Marxist themes of class struggles and social emancipation, recognition struggles have to do with aspirations to freedom and justice connected to gender, sexuality, race and national recognition. Therefore, while Cox focuses on contemporary redistri-bution struggles, Linklater turns to questions of identity and community as more significant than economic relations in today's quest for emancipation.

Cox sets out to challenge realism's assumptions, namely the study of interstate relations in isolation from other social forces. He stresses the need to see global politics as a collective construction evolving through the complex interplay of state, sub-state and trans-state forces in economic, cultural and ideological spheres. His purpose is to pay attention to the whole range of spheres where change is needed in contemporary global politics. For example, when realism focuses only on great powers and strategic stability, it ends up reinforcing a set of unjust global relations stemming from power and coercion. For this reason, Cox challenges the idea that 'truth' is absolute – as in realism's assertion that there is a timeless logic to international relations, or liberalism's assertion that the pursuit of global capitalism is positive. Instead, he asserts that 'theory is always for someone and for some purpose' (Cox

1981, 128). Drawing on Gramsci, Cox comes up with a picture of the world political system brought into being by the hegemony and hierarchies of power manufactured in the economic arena. Therefore, power is understood in the context of a set of globalised relations of production demanding the transformation of the nation-state, and depends on the combination of material elements and ideas for acquiring legitimacy (Cox and Jacobsen 1977). Cox explores the economic contradictions spurring change in power relations and guiding transitions towards a fairer world order, even if acknowledging that emancipation is not inevitable.

As Hutchings (2001) points out, the critical project connecting Linklater to Cox sets out to uncover all sorts of hegemonic interests feeding the world order as a first step to overcome global systems of exclusion and inequality. Linklater's critical project aims at reconstructing cosmopolitanism, drawing not from some abstract or utopian moral principle but from non-instrumental action and ideal speech (open and non-coercive communication) assumptions developed by Habermas. Ideal speech is the critical tool used in the reconstruction of political communities (from local to global levels) through open dialogue and non-coercive communication, a process whereby all affected by political decisions put forward their claims and justify them on the basis of rational and universally accepted principles of validity. This method poses questions of the 'good life' (what a society ought to be like) and questions of justice (fairness in the way members of a society choose what their society ought to be like).

Thus, emancipation is conceived not with reference to an abstract universal idea but based on a process of open discussion about who can be excluded legitimately from specific political arrangements and what kinds of particularities (gender, race, language) entitle people to special sets of rights. For Linklater, the historical development of citizenship attests to both the potential and the limitations of such a process of open discussion about rights – who is entitled to what in the context of the state system. Citizenship has been the critical concept and set of practices permitting the enjoyment of universal rights inside a community (freedom of conscience, freedom of movement, freedom of association), but also the protection of vulnerable minorities by granting them particular rights in order to avoid or mitigate the effects of discrimination. On the other hand, however, citizenship has divided humanity into national groupings and has therefore been a barrier to the universal fulfilment of human freedom.

According to Linklater then, emancipation demands global interactions guided by open, inclusive and non-coercive dialogue about the ties that bind communities together. This also extends to our obligations to strangers and how fair it is to restrict outsiders from the enjoyment of rights granted to insiders. For Linklater, the answer lies in the potential for a more universal concept of citizenship, refashioned through open dialogue among those affected by the global processes that are changing the world. These processes are issues like non-state forms of violence (such as sexual violence and terrorism), forced migration, climate change and resource depletion. Therefore, critical theory can be seen as an instrument of the powerless to advance more equitable types of global relations. More importantly for us, within IR theory it combats the traditional approaches, mainly liberalism and realism, and shines a light on how they feed the imbalances of an unjust global order by failing to question (or critique) their foundational claims. Linklater's work is marked by the awareness that modernity is an unfinished project in its potential for accomplishing human freedom, namely through the transformation of the competitive system of separate states into a global community.

By admitting that immediate security needs press humans to set up bounded communities and to act according to national loyalties, Linklater recognises the limits to cosmopolitan politics. At the same time however, he underlines that there is a growing awareness that global interconnectedness and vulnerabilities impose their consequences on how communities define themselves and live side by side with others. Proximity with strangers prompts, for instance, a heightened sense of sharing a finite planet and finite resources and leads individuals to question exclusive obligations to the state in favour of a degree of cosmopolitan responsibility towards those who do not belong to one's national community.

Accordingly, Linklater explores the moral tensions emerging between humanity and citizenship ('humans' and 'citizens') in order to devise practical possibilities for creating more inclusive communities, with a civilising effect upon the conduct of international relations. Linklater does not underestimate the historical movement towards the creation of bounded moral communities (nation-states) but also sees potential within the historical process to enhance the expansion of rights and duties beyond the state. The fact that it has been possible for states in the modern international system to agree upon the protection of human rights and the political relevance of avoiding human wrongs is a sign of the relevance of these ideas.

What unites critical theorists like Cox, Linklater and others, then, is a political inquiry with an explicit emancipatory purpose. It aims at uncovering the potential for a fairer system of global relations resulting from already existing principles, practices and communities that expands human rights and pre-vents harm to strangers.

Critical theory and the European migrant 'crisis'

Haman stares at the long night behind him when I surprise his absent gaze on the deck of the Blue Star ferry carrying us to the Greek port of Piraeus. Departing from Rhodes, the ferry had made its first stop at the island of Kos where dozens of refugees from the Syrian war lined up patiently for hours and eventually got a place on board. Haman was one of them. After talking for hours about the war and his expectations for the future, it was clear to me that ferry on the Aegean Sea was a metaphor of a global community plagued with obstacles to human freedom but holding the resources for its fulfilment. After Kos though, I could not really tell anymore who was a tourist and who was a refugee, who was Greek or Athenian and who was neither – and it occurred to me why these categories had to matter at all. The common human condition aboard the ferry would stand for the night, but the following morning tourists would continue their tranquil journey home while refugees would have to improvise their way across Europe, begging for hospitality. At the port of Piraeus, on that early morning of August 2015, I said goodbye to Haman and wished him luck for the journey. It is Friday and he knows he must reach the Hungarian border before Tuesday or risk being trapped by the fence erected hastily in the previous days to block migrants on the Serbian side. 'It'll be cold' he says, in a premonition of what lay ahead for those like him seeking refuge in Europe. That was the last I heard from Haman. I stayed there for a while, looking at him blending into the crowd conveyed throughout Europe as a crisis of refugees and illegal migrants.

This brief encounter with Haman and his story is a trigger for recalling how in recent years increasing numbers of people escaping persecution, war and famine have tried to reach safe havens like Europe. While this has been approached mostly as a 'crisis' affecting Europe and the national communities composing it, some voices have underlined how the history of humanity has always been a history of migration, peaceful or otherwise, and that today more people than at any time since the Second World War are being displaced from their homes. A critical perspective assumes that the security claims of refugees fleeing war-torn countries constitute a cosmopolitan responsibility for the whole of humankind, especially for those with the resources to address them. It proceeds by critiquing security arrangements pleading exclusive loyalty to a bounded community and refusing refugees a number of cosmopolitan rights (hospitality and refuge). The point is not simply to understand how the world is constituted by moral tensions opposing nationals to strangers, but to contribute to more equitable political solutions to the current refugee 'crisis' by taking to the negotiating table the most vulnerable and their legitimate security concerns. Contrary to more traditional theories, critical theory does not see refugees as apart from the violence and inequality that produce them. In fact, it sets out to locate current waves of forced migration in the context of deeper economic and geopolitical structures producing harm and exclusion in a globalising world. Along the Cox/Linklater axis, current migration must be seen as forced upon individuals and the by-product of the current world order. The state of these relations excludes the potential for human understanding and mutual recognition, as it has come about through the harmful globalisation of production and connected dynamics of nation-building, war and environmental degradation. Therefore, a critical perspective inquires deeper into how global economic forces, and related hierarchies of power, become complicit in creating the chaos and insecurity forcing people to leave their homes in different parts of the world. This entails looking in particular to how the dynamics of global capitalism are producing failed states throughout Africa and the Middle East, not just as an unintended misfortune but as part of how power itself works.

The main challenge for critical theory then is to connect theory to practice, to be able to set up a theoretical lens that results in a real-world transformative outcome. It is not enough to understand and trace the origins of harm and displacement in the world; it is crucial to use that understanding to reach fairer security arrangements that do not neglect refugees' claims to basic rights. Someone wanting to pursue a critical line of inquiry about the refugee 'crisis' might want to start with Haman and his journey from Syria to Europe as a mirror image of the current plight of so many people in the Global South. For critical theory today, politics, knowledge and global orders are for people like Haman and should serve the purpose of freeing them from unnecessary harm and unfair or unbalanced globalised interactions. Institutions like the state must be assessed in terms of how they fare in overcoming various types of exclusion vis-à-vis insiders and outsiders. Critical theory, more than other approaches, promises to go deeper in understanding why refugees have to leave their homes. This entails producing knowledge about direct reasons (war in Syria or elsewhere) but also about global structures of power and harm as well as the agents complicit in it (broader geopolitical interests, the workings of the global economy, climate change and its effects over the lives of communities). Moreover, critical theory examines the moral consequences (what must be done) of Haman's journey and what kind of responsibility others might bear for Haman's plight.

Cosmopolitan in character, critical theory refuses to see states as bounded moral communities by nature and instead finds in them the potential to protect strangers in need and include them in a broader notion of national interest. In the context of the current refugee 'crisis', critique is directed to the different norms and practices approved by states vis-à-vis incoming refugees. A basic move is to distinguish which ones are and which are not compatible with cosmopolitan duties already enshrined in international law and upheld by many people and organisations in different societies. A second move is to promote civic initiatives capable of consolidating fairer and more balanced relations (solutions to the 'crisis') between those who seek refuge from harm and those who are in a position to guarantee protection from harm. Solutions must be sought in open dialogue, resorting to rational arguments that take into consideration everyone's concerns and interests. Leaving solutions to national governments alone is not an option due to their rather strict position on national interests. On the contrary, a more balanced position would result from the active involvement of civil society, local authorities, European authorities and refugees themselves. After all, Europe is a pertinent case here as it is the home of the European Union – a project that united the bulk of European states in a supranational, and relatively open-bordered, union in which all citizens are legally free to work and live wherever they please within the Union. Clearly, there is an existing framework within European politics to work with to reach a more just solution to the migration 'crisis' than the one advanced by those nations who closed their borders. The reward for someone following a critical line of inquiry is therefore to understand to the full that theory is always implicated in practice and that the way we conceive the refugee 'crisis' shapes the kind of solution we envisage for it. From a critical perspective, then, there is only a true solution to this 'crisis' when political actors embrace cosmopolitan criteria that balance the whole range of interests and respect the rights of everyone involved.

Conclusion

Recognising that there are very different strands of thought within critical theory, this chapter has narrowed its approach to introduce critical theory as a specific line of inquiry seeking to advance emancipation, or human freedom, in the conduct of global affairs. A relevant critique seeks to trace forms of exclusion that instigate both redistribution and recognition struggles and then identify the potential for progressive change inspired by immanent ideas, norms and practices. From a critical perspective, then, people – not states – must be put at the centre of politics, global or otherwise. Additionally, political arrangements should be judged, or critiqued, according to their capacity to advance emancipation and the broadening of moral boundaries. Critical theory assumes an active role in the betterment of human affairs according to the potential for freedom inherent in modernity and the identification of political alternatives at hand in the globalising society and the historical process bringing it into being.

7

Poststructuralism

AISHLING MC MORROW

Poststructuralism encourages a way of looking at the world that challenges what comes to be accepted as 'truth' and 'knowledge'. Poststructuralists always call into question how certain accepted 'facts' and 'beliefs' actually work to reinforce the dominance and power of particular actors within international relations. Poststructuralism doubts the possibility of attaining universal laws or truths as there is no world that exists independently of our own interpretations. This viewpoint is underscored by Foucault's (1984, 127) assertion that 'we must not imagine the world turns towards us a legible face which we would only have to decipher'. For this reason, poststructuralists encourage researchers to be sceptical of universal narratives that attempt to offer an objective worldview, as these assumptions are heavily influenced by pre-existing assumptions of what is true – and usually underlined by the views of those in power. This renders poststructuralism openly critical of any theory that claims to be able to identify objective fact – as truth and knowledge are subjective entities that are *produced* rather than *discovered*. Therefore, by design, poststructuralism conflicts with the bulk of other IR theories as it finds them unable (or unwilling) to fully account for the true diversity of international relations.

The basics of poststructuralism

Poststructuralists argue that 'knowledge' comes to be accepted as such due to the power and prominence of certain actors in society known as 'elites', who then impose it upon others. Elites take on a range of forms and occupy many different roles in contemporary society. For instance, they include government ministers who decide policy focus and direction for a state, business leaders who leverage vast financial resources to shape market direction, and media outlets that decide how a person is portrayed while reporting a story. Additionally, elites are often also categorised as 'experts' within society, giving them the authority to further reinforce the viewpoints that serve their best interests to a wide audience. Jenny Edkins (2006) uses the example of famines to show that when elite actors refer to famine as a natural disaster, they are removing the event from its political context. Therefore, the ways that famines occur as a result of elites taking particular forms of political action, through processes of exploitation or inaction due to profits on increased food prices, are lost when they are presented as unavoidable natural disasters.

Although great emphasis and focus is placed upon the authority of the elite actors to decide what we count as valid knowledge and assumptions within society, poststructuralism asserts that the way in which this power is achieved is through the manipulation of discourse. Discourses facilitate the process by which certain information comes to be accepted as unquestionable truth. Discourses which augment the power of elites are called *dominant* or *official* discourses by poststructuralists. The strength of dominant discourses lies in their ability to shut out other options or opinions to the extent that thinking outside the realms set by the discourse is seen as irrational.

An example of this can be found in the security versus liberty debate. The wish to increase security levels across society – in response to crime, irregular migration and terrorist threats – has been presented as a sliding scale whereby if a state wishes to be secure then the public must endure a reduction in personal freedoms. Personal freedoms – such as the freedom of expression and freedom of assembly – have been placed as the limit against which security exists. In this discursive construct, then, people are presented with the choice between a state that respects civil liberties but is left potentially insecure or a state that must curb personal freedoms in order to be secure and protected. In practice, the dominant discourse of securing the state often works to silence any concerns about enhanced state power. An elite programme to restrict civil liberties can be justified to a society conditioned by the 'expert' repetition of this discourse by appealing to the objective logic it asserts and discounting all other interpretations. Therefore, the move to achieve increased levels of security *without* the infringement upon personal or civil liberties is excluded from the argument, as the two are constantly being positioned in direct opposition to each other.

For poststructuralists, language is one of the most crucial elements for the creation and perpetuation of a dominant discourse. Through language, certain actors, concepts and events are placed in hierarchical pairs, named binary oppositions, whereby one element of the set is favoured over the other in order to create or perpetuate meaning. The power relation that is embedded within this relationship (for example, good versus evil or developed versus undeveloped) serves to reinforce the preferred meaning within the discursive construct. International Relations as a discipline is full of these oppositions and they are used by elites to both create favourable meaning out of certain events and to allow for this meaning to be easily absorbed and accepted by the wider public. One of the most common binary oppositions is to establish different groups or countries in terms of 'them' versus 'us'.

If we look to the aftermath of the events of 11 September 2001 (commonly known as 9/11) we can see these categories of differentiation and their influence begin to manifest themselves. President George W. Bush described Iran, Iraq and North Korea as an 'axis of evil' – making these countries the 'them' that were rhetorically and politically positioned as international pariahs in contrast to the innocent 'us' of the United States and its allies. Hence, this binary opposition enabled Bush to claim that the United States was opposite to all that this trio represented and would be justified in taking various actions during a global campaign against states that were judged to sponsor, or harbour, terrorists.

If we look to the work of one of the leading scholars of poststructuralism, Michel Foucault, then the concepts of elites, discourses and the power of language and binary oppositions all tie together to create what he labels a 'regime of truth'. This model applies to the ruling discourse that operates unquestioned within society, masquerading as the truth or fact. A regime of truth, then, is constituted by the dominant discourse, elite actors and the language that is used to create and sustain meaning and truth that serves the interest of the favoured actors.

The importance of poststructuralism is to highlight existing regimes of truth and show that conventional ways of thinking and analysis in international relations are unable to point out how certain other possibilities are excluded by these discourses from the very start. Butler (2003) builds upon this idea of discourses excluding other possibilities by proposing that certain lives, in certain conflicts or terrorist atrocities, are deemed as more 'grievable' than others. Butler argues that thousands of people are lost to conflict in countries such as Palestine and Afghanistan, often at the hands of Western powers, and yet these people are not mourned or memorialised or even heard of within Western reports of war.

This hierarchy of grief can also be seen in the outpouring of sympathy for victims of terrorist attacks in Paris in November 2015 and Nice in July 2016. Yet, similar attacks in Beirut and Nigeria in November 2015 and Baghdad in July 2016 (to name but a few) went largely unnoticed and were silenced within regimes of truth that mourned for, or favoured, the 'innocent' Western victim.

Poststructuralism and media representations of terrorists

The media is a prime example of a site where discourses within regimes of truth are (re)produced and can be identified. How we receive information and the way that news events are presented to a society shapes how we conceptualise and react to political events. As such, if we want to observe how people have come to conceive and frame both terrorism and terrorists, the poststructuralist can analyse media accounts in order to analyse the discursive construction of these political actors and associated terrorist events.

As the defining global terrorist attack of the twenty-first century, the attacks of 11 September 2001 on the United States can be used to convey how dominant discourses, instigated by governmental elites, were perpetuated and reinforced by the media.

In newspaper reports – specifically, in the week after the attacks – the terrorists were presented as evil and irrational, their stated political motivations were effaced and instead terrorists were repeatedly spoken of as crazed and apolitical. The terrorists were plagued by 'inexplicable neurosis' and driven by 'ethnic, superstitious and tribal madnesses' (Toynbee 2001). Additionally, these terrorists were set apart as different from more traditional forms of terrorism that the world had previously witnessed through the highlighting of the lethality and deadliness of mass murdering transnational terrorism – a move which heightened the emotions of fear and anxiety further.

To underscore this link to death and destruction, the media narrative also consistently linked both the acts and actors of 9/11 to images and metaphors of pestilence and disease. In contrast to this, was the cultivation of the idea of 'American innocence' (Boswell 2001) that was 'vulnerable to hate' (Boyd 2001), coupled with the persistent repetition and reminder of the suffering of the victims of 9/11 and the heroism of the first responders. Interspersed with this, the widespread international outcry to the attacks simultaneously worked to further emphasise the immorality and inhumanity of these actors. Themes of patriotism and civility were deployed within the media to further distance the cohesive 'us' from the generic barbarian terrorist. The reactions of the public that gathered together to pray, support each other, volunteer and eventually join the military juxtaposed radically with the destructive actions of the terrorists. Moreover, the emotions that the narratives of these actions evoked related back to feelings of love, empathy and altruism that the media utilised to engender further cohesion in society against the 'other' of the terrorist.

The importance of the recognition of this discourse is *not* to attempt to present these political actors – the terrorists – in a better light, but to recognise how the consistent and universal portrayal of them as evil and irrational made certain reactions and foreign policy actions more amenable and immediately cut off other methods of responding to these terrorist attacks. From this, poststructuralism critically questions what purpose did the construction, by both the media and the government, of a dominant discourse that posited the terrorists and the society that they belonged to as evil and barbaric serve? How did the positing of an unbridgeable chasm between the civilised society and the primeval terrorist, within this regime of truth, favour elite agendas? One answer has been the identification of how this 'good versus evil' construct prepared and almost rallied the American public for war. It certainly prevented the chance of dealing with these attacks through diplomacy, as the overarching discourse stated that these terrorists merely wanted to destroy the world before them. While some may support the wars in Afghanistan (2001) and Iraq (2003) that followed these attacks, the poststructuralist contribution deconstructs how this militaristic and aggressive response to 9/11 was legitimised by the discursive construction of the terrorists, the emotions that were manipulated and the divide between 'us' and 'them' that was fashioned.

The pervasion of this discourse also served to conflate the motivations and acts of these terrorists with the construction of a wider Muslim and Arab society. With the simplistic interpretation of the historical relations between the 'West' and 'East' that was encouraged in this discursive construction, the regime of truth played upon and amplified the notion of the Muslim or Arab world as backward and primordial. Within the regime of truth of the War on Terror, then, this emotive discourse was extended to every Muslim, every Arab, and, eventually, every non-Westerner.

With the passage of time, we are also able to trace the gradual disruption to and destabilising of this regime of truth. As the United States was drawn further into destructive and protracted conflicts in Afghanistan and Iraq, the public opinion that had supported intervention began to wane. Over time, the discursive construction of terrorists by the media was not strong enough to override the concurrent media accounts of large numbers of casualties resulting from the intervention. Along with these fatalities, as the media began to report on the abuses that were carried out, the regime of truth that had been centred on the foreign policy directives of the Bush presidency started to falter. Thus, the official discourse regarding terrorism and intervention was changing and this shift can be identified by a shift to more clandestine forms of intervention in the Middle East from 2009 onwards – watermarked by the presidency of Barack Obama. The increased use of special forces and drone strikes allowed Obama to continue to exert influence over the region without overtly declaring war – while also distancing his administration from the military intervention that defined that of his predecessor.

The official discourse across an event, although powerful, never fully accounts for the reading of the entire situation. While the presentation of terrorists as irrational and evil has found solid ground and the dominant perceptions of terrorism and terrorists are of an illogical and apolitical act and actor, there always will be deviation from this conceptualisation. As such, the official discourse as crafted by elites never fully accounts for or subsumes the whole of a society. For example, despite the warmongering in the wake of 9/11, there were large-scale anti-war protests by members of the public across many nations. This messy entanglement of the everyday and the elite shows that a plethora of discourses can coexist and craft the view of international relations that we are offered. From this we must recognise that elite and everyday discourses co-exist and, although one assumes a dominant position, there are still many other competing discourses at play that shape international relations and have the potential to contribute to understandings commonly seen as 'knowledge' and 'truth'.

Conclusion

The impact of poststructuralism within IR theory comes from its ability to not only identify and uncover power relations that dictate political events but also make space for alternative discourses to emerge that can also affect the course of events. By examining elite actors, we can see how commonly accepted facts about the political system are not 'natural' but, instead, constructed in order to favour a dominant discourse. Furthermore, by tracing the rise and fall of regimes of truth as they take on new forms and favour new actors, poststructuralism shows how discourses can change over time and be destabilised. Most importantly, poststructuralism allows you to become carefully attuned to – and interrogate – the many ways that power is exercised.

8

Feminism

SARAH SMITH

From the outset, feminist theory has challenged women's near complete absence from traditional IR theory and practice. This absence is visible both in women's marginalisation from decision-making and in the assumption that the reality of women's day-to-day lives is not impacted by or important to international relations. Beyond this, feminist contributions to IR can also be understood through their deconstruction of gender – both as socially const-ructed identities and as a powerful organising logic. This means recognising and then challenging assumptions about masculine and feminine gender roles that dictate what both women and men should or can do in global politics and what counts as important in considerations of international relations. These assumptions in turn shape the process of global politics and the impacts these have on men and women's lives. Rather than suggest that traditional IR was gender-neutral – that is, that gender and IR were two separate spheres that did not impact on each other – feminist theory has shown that traditional IR is in fact gender-blind. Feminist scholarship therefore takes both women and gender seriously – and in doing so it challenges IR's foundational concepts and assumptions.

The basics of feminism

If we start with feminism's first contribution – making women visible – an early contribution of feminist theorists is revealing that women were and are routinely exposed to gendered violence. In making violence against women visible, an international system that tacitly accepted a large amount of violence against women as a normal state of affairs was also exposed. For example, former UN Secretary General Ban Ki-moon's 'UNiTE' campaign to end violence against women estimated that up to seven out of ten women will experience violence at some point in their lives – and that approximately 600 million women live in countries where domestic violence is not yet considered a crime. Violence against women is prevalent globally and is not specific to any particular political or economic system. Jacqui True (2012) has demonstrated the links between violence against women in the private sphere (for example, domestic violence) and the kinds of violence women experience in public, in an increasingly globalised workplace and in times of war. In short, nowhere do women share the same economic, political or social rights as men and everywhere there are prevalent forms of gendered violence, whether this be domestic violence in the home or sexual violence in conflict. In looking at violence against women in such a way, it is possible to see a continuum of gendered violence that does not reflect neat and distinct categories of peace, stability and so on. Many societies are thought of as predominantly peaceful or stable despite high levels of violence against a particular portion of the population. It also presents a very different image of violence and insecurity to that viewed through the security agendas of states, which is characteristic of traditional IR viewpoints.

In making women visible, feminism has also highlighted women's absence from decision-making and institutional structures. For example, in 2015 the World Bank estimated that globally women made up just 22.9% of national parliaments. One of the core assumptions of traditional perspectives that feminism has challenged is the exclusionary focus on areas that are considered 'high' politics – for example, sovereignty, the state and military security. The traditional focus on states and relations between them overlooks the fact that men are predominantly in charge of state institutions, dominating power and decision-making structures. It also ignores other areas that both impact global politics and are impacted by it. This is a gendered exclusion as women contribute in essential ways to global politics even though they are more likely to populate those areas not considered high politics and their day-to-day lives may be considered peripheral. Traditional perspectives that ignore gender not only overlook the contributions of women and the impact global politics has on them but also perpetually justify this exclusion. If women are outside these domains of power, then their experiences and contributions are not relevant. Feminist theorists have worked to demonstrate that this distinction between private and public is false. In doing so they show that previously excluded areas are central to the functioning of IR, even if they are not acknowledged, and that the exclusion and inclusion of certain areas in traditional IR thinking is based on gendered ideas of what counts and does not count.

This brings us to the second key contribution of feminism – exposing and deconstructing socially constructed gender norms. In making sense of IR in a way that takes both women and gender seriously, feminism has demonstrated the construction of gendered identities that perpetuate normative ideas of what men and women should do. In this regard, it is important to understand the distinction between 'sex' as biological and 'gender' as socially constructed. Not all gender considerations rest on the analysis of women, nor should they, and gender relates to expectations and identities attached to both men and women. Gender is understood as the socially constructed assumptions that are assigned to either male or female bodies – that is, behaviour that is assumed to be appropriate 'masculine' (male) or 'feminine' (female) behaviour. Masculinity is often associated with rationality, power, independence and the public sphere. Femininity is often associated with irrationality, in need of protection, domesticity and the private sphere. These socially and politically produced gender identities shape and influence global interactions, and IR as theory – and global politics as practice – also produces such gendered identities in perpetuating assumptions about who should do what and why. These gender identities are also imbued with power, in particular patriarchal power, which subordinates women and feminine gender identities to men and masculine gender identities. What this means is that socially constructed gender identities also determine distributions of power, which impact where women are in global politics. Whereas men can be feminine and women masculine, masculinity is expected for men and femininity of women.

Cynthia Enloe (1989) asked the question 'where are the women?', encouraging IR scholars to see the spaces that women inhabit in global politics and demonstrating that women are essential actors in the international system. She focused on deconstructing the distinctions between what is considered international and what is considered personal, showing how global politics impacts on and is shaped by the daily activities of men and women – and in turn how these activities rest on gendered identities. Traditionally, the military and war making have been seen as masculine endeavours, linked with the idea that men are warriors and protectors, that they are legitimate armed actors who fight to protect those in need of protection – women, children and non-fighting men. In practice this has meant that the many ways that women contribute to conflict and experience conflict have been considered peripheral, outside the realm of IR's considerations. For example, the issue of sexual and gendered violence in conflict has only recently entered the international agenda. Comparatively, the mass rape of women during and after the Second World War was not prosecuted as the occurrence was either considered an unfortunate by-product of war or simply ignored. This has since changed, with the 2002 Rome Statute recognising rape as a war crime. However, this recognition has not led to the curtailment of conflict related sexual violence and this form of violence remains endemic in many conflicts around the world, as does impunity for its occurrence.

In turn, these issues highlight the importance of intersectionality – understanding that IR is shaped not only by gender but also by other identities, such as class, race or ethnicity. Intersectionality refers to where these identities intersect, and in turn how different groups of people are marginalised, suggesting that we must consider each in tandem rather than in isolation. In examining wartime rape, Lori Handrahan (2004, 437) has shown the intersection of gender and ethnic identities, where the enemy's women become constructed as 'other' and violence against them consequently comes to represent the 'expansion of ethnic territory by the male conqueror.' This rests on gendered constructions, which occur at the intersections with other forms of identity, such as ethnicity or race. Gendered constructions that see women characterised as protected mean that conquering them – through rape or sexual violence – is representative of power and domination over one's enemy. Applying feminist theory to the issue of male wartime rape also shows the gendered logics that inform its occurrence, in particular that the rape of male opponents is seen to 'feminise' (that is, humiliate, defeat) opponents. This again highlights the contribution of feminism in understanding how gender influences IR and how the feminine is undervalued or devalued.

As discussed above, feminism has exposed gender violence and women's marginalisation in global politics. However, it also challenges gendered constructions of women as inherently peaceful, as in need of protection or as victims. Feminists see these constructions as further evidence of gender inequality and also as contributing to the exclusion of women from traditional IR perspectives in the first instance. If women are assumed to be victims rather than actors or as peaceful rather than aggressive or as only existing in the domestic or private realm (rather than the public sphere), then their experiences and perspectives on global politics are more easily ignored and justified as marginal. Accounts of women disrupting these gender identities, such as being agents of political violence for example, have challenged these assumptions. This is an important contribution of feminism and one that challenges the construction of gendered identities that do not reflect the diversity of women's engagements with IR and in practice perpetuate women's limited access to power. Therefore, taking feminism seriously is not simply about upending the historical marginalisation of women, it also provides a more complete picture of global politics by taking into account a broader range of actors and actions.

Feminism and peacekeeping

Building peace after conflict is an increasingly central concern of IR scholars – especially as conflicts become broader and more complex. There are also questions regarding how post-conflict societies are to be rebuilt and how best to prevent relapses into conflict. Peacekeeping missions are one way that the international community seeks to institute sustainable peace after conflict and the United Nation's traditional peacekeeping role (understood as acting as an impartial interlocutor or monitor) has broadened considerably. Missions now frequently include a laundry list of state-building roles, including re-establishing police and military forces and building political institutions. Feminist theorists have demonstrated the ways that peacekeeping, as security-seeking behaviour, is shaped by masculine notions of militarised security. Post-conflict situations are generally characterised as the formal cessation of violence between armed combatants, ideally transitioning to a situation where the state has a monopoly on the use of force. It is this shift that peacekeeping missions seek to facilitate, conducting a wide range of tasks such as disarming combatants, facilitating peace deals between various state and non-state groups, monitoring elections and building rule of law capacity in state institutions such as police forces and the military.

However, as feminist IR scholars have shown, violence against women often continues in the post-conflict period at rates commensurate to or even greater than during the conflict period. This includes rape and sexual assault, domestic violence and forced prostitution, as well as those selling sex to alleviate financial insecurity. The dominant approach to keeping peace often obscures these kinds of violence. Issues like gender equality and domestic violence (and human rights) are considered 'soft' issues as opposed to the 'hard' or real issues of military security. This understanding of peace, then, is one in which women's security is not central.

In terms of structural and indirect violence, women are generally excluded from positions of power and decision-making in reconstruction efforts and have limited access to economic resources. Donna Pankhurst (2008) has theorised what she terms a post-conflict backlash against women, one that is chiefly characterised by high rates of violence and restrictions on women's access to political, economic and social resources post-conflict. The restriction of women's access to such resources – such as basic food, housing and education – makes them more susceptible to gendered violence. This often begins with women's exclusion from peace negotiations and deals, which instead focus on elite actors who are predominantly men, often militarised men. In peacekeeping missions, women are also under-represented. In 1993, women made up only 1% of deployed personnel. That figure had only risen to 3% for military and 10% for policy personnel by 2014. As gender inequality has become increasingly acknowledged, those involved in peacekeeping have paid more attention to the causes and consequences of women's insecurity in post-conflict settings.

In October 2000 the UN Security Council devoted an entire session to Women, Peace and Security – adopting Resolution 1325 as a result. This resolution called for a gender perspective to be 'mainstreamed' throughout peace operations and for women to be included in peace agreements and post-conflict decision-making – in addition to the protection of women and girls during conflict. Resolution 1325 calls on all actors to recognise the 'special needs' of women and girls in post-conflict societies, to support local women's peace initiatives, and advocates for the protection of women's human rights in electoral, judiciary and police systems. However, consistent with the construction of a gendered understanding of peace discussed above, there remain limitations to the full implementation of Resolution 1325.

A United Nations study by Radhika Coomaraswamy (2015) found that gender in peacekeeping continues to be under-resourced politically and financially, and the gendered elements of post-conflict reconstruction are still marginalised in missions. Women still experience high rates of violence post-conflict, are still excluded from peace processes and still ignored in peace-building policy. This is demonstrated, for example, in national and international attempts to disarm former combatants after conflict and reintegrate them into post-conflict society. This is a post-conflict policy area that feminist scholars have routinely exposed as being highly gendered and exclusionary of women who are former combatants. Megan Mackenzie (2010) has attributed this to constructed gender identities that minimise the idea that women are agents in conflict or involved in war-making, instead constructing them as victims with limited agency. In other words, they are subject to war rather than war's actors.

This means not only that women are excluded from disarmament programmes because of socially produced gender norms but also that they are unable to access the material and economic benefits that may flow from such programmes – or the political and social gains they could make from being recognised as legitimate veterans in post-conflict societies. This example demonstrates the power invested in gendered identities, the ways they can shape policy and how gender inequality is perpetuated via such policy.

Finally, international interventions such as peacekeeping missions also contribute to the continuation of violence post-conflict and are a site in which gendered identities are produced. There have been numerous reports of peacekeepers perpetrating sexual violence against women, girls and boys while on mission. This issue gained much attention in 2015 and into 2016, when a United Nations whistle blower exposed not only reports of sexual abuse of children in the Central African Republic by French peacekeepers but also the United Nation's inaction in the face of these reports. From a feminist perspective, the impunity that peacekeepers enjoy – despite rhetorical commitments to zero tolerance – is a result of gendered security imperatives in which militarised security and the coherence of the institution (whether that be an international organisation or a state) is prioritised over the welfare of the individual.

Conclusion

Feminist research has demonstrated the value in taking women's experiences and contributions seriously and used that as a base to demonstrate how IR rests on, and perpetuates, gendered ideas about who does what, who experiences what – and why – in global politics. Beyond this there is also recognition that women are important agents in political, economic and social processes. Despite its designation, feminism does more than focus on women, or what are considered women's issues. In highlighting both inequality and relations of power, feminism reveals gendered power and what it does in global politics. Being concerned with women's subordination to men, gendered inequality and the construction of gendered identities, feminism has challenged a homogenous concept of 'women' in IR and exposed gendered logics as powerful organising frameworks.

9

Postcolonialism

SHEILA NAIR

Postcolonialism examines how societies, governments and peoples in the formerly colonised regions of the world experience international relations. The use of 'post' by postcolonial scholars by no means suggests that the effects or impacts of colonial rule are now long gone. Rather, it highlights the impact that colonial and imperial histories still have in shaping a colonial way of thinking about the world and how Western forms of knowledge and power marginalise the non-Western world. Postcolonialism is not only interested in understanding the world as it is, but also as it ought to be. It is concerned with the disparities in global power and wealth accumulation and why some states and groups exercise so much power over others. By raising issues such as this, postcolonialism asks different questions to the other theories of IR and allows for not just alternative readings of history but also alternative perspectives on contemporary events and issues.

The basics of postcolonialism

Postcolonialism has specifically drawn attention to IR theory's neglect of the critical intersections of empire, race/ethnicity, gender and class (among other factors) in the workings of global power that reproduce a hierarchical IR. This hierarchy is centred not on striving for a more equal distribution of power among peoples and states but on the concentration of power.

A key theme to postcolonialism is that Western perceptions of the non-West are a result of the legacies of European colonisation and imperialism. Discourses – primarily things that are written or spoken – constructed non-Western states and peoples as 'other' or different to the West, usually in a way that made them appear to be inferior. In doing so, they helped European powers justify their domination over other peoples in the name of bringing civilisation or progress.

To better understand postcolonialism we can consider the discourses that make certain power relations seem natural or even inevitable. Postcolonialism views key issues in International Relations as constituting discourses of power. This notion of a discourse allows scholars to utilise a frame of reference for thinking about the world and its problems that does not merely reside in the empirically verifiable and 'fact'-based inquiry that drives traditional IR theories such as realism and liberalism. Take, for example, the issue of global inequality. Postcolonialism suggests that in order to better understand how global class relations emerge and are maintained we must address ideas about why these relations appear normal. This approach points to how characterisations of global poverty are often accompanied by images and narratives of non-Western governments and societies as simultaneously primitive, hyper-masculine, aggressive, childlike and effeminate. In short, postcolonialism argues that addressing and finding solutions to poverty and global inequality come up against representations of the other that make it difficult for Western policymakers to shed their biases and address the underlying global structural factors such as how capital and resources are accumulated and flow around the world generating inequality. For this reason, solutions often focus only on intervening to support a seemingly less developed state, rather than addressing the underlying causes of global inequality.

In analysing how key concepts such as power, the state and security serve to reproduce the status quo, postcolonialism proposes a more complex view of such concepts than is characteristic of traditional theories. For example, the concept of sovereignty, and with it the contours of the modern state, were imposed on the colonial world by European powers. Yet it is a concept that is usually taken for granted by scholars of realism and liberalism. Postcolonialism also challenges the Marxist perspective that class struggle is at the root of historical change – instead demonstrating how *race* shapes history. Analyses that focus only on class fail to consider how the identification of the 'Third World' (a term developed during the Cold War to describe those states unaligned to the United States or the Soviet Union) as 'backward', 'primitive' or 'non-rational' are linked to persistent economic marginalisation. Similarly, while mainstream IR theories see the international system as an anarchy, postcolonial scholars see it as a hierarchy. Colonialism and imperialism fostered a long process of continued domination of the West over the rest of the world and cultural, economic and political domination still characterise global politics.

Postcolonialism also demonstrates how Western views about Islam and its adherents are a manifestation of the West's own insecurities. The rise of political Islam across the Muslim world – watermarked by Iran's Islamic Revolution in 1979 – not only confronted neo-imperialist interventions but also revealed the impacts of core cultural and social shifts accompanying a more interconnected global economy. In the West, however, the view of this resurgence has been interpreted by prominent policymakers and academics as heralding a 'clash of civilizations' (Huntington 1993) and worse, constituting a direct threat to Western civilization. Edward Said (1997) showed how Western media, film, academia and policy elites rely on a distorted lens or framework used to describe the history and culture of Arab peoples and adherents of Islam. He called it Orientalism because it constructs a particular idea of the so-called 'Orient' that is distinct from the West and that in a binary or dualistic way of thinking ascribes to the Orient and its inhabitants characteristics that are essentially the opposite of the West. For instance, people of the Orient may be characterised as being exotic, emotional, feminine, backward, hedonistic, non-rational and so forth. This is in contrast to the more positive attributes usually associated with the West such as rationality, masculinity, civilization and modernity.

Many postcolonial scholars emphasise how orientalist discourses are still visible in Western representations today. Representations and perceptions matter to postcolonial theorists because they dictate what comes to be seen as normal or as making sense.

Postcolonialism owes a significant debt to Edward Said for his work on developing Orientalism. Yet Said himself was influenced by the writing of anti-colonial and nationalist thinkers such as Frantz Fanon (1967) and Albert Memmi (1991) whose works discuss the power of 'othering'. For example, Fanon shows how race shapes the way that the coloniser relates to the colonised and vice versa by capturing how some people under colonial rule began to internalise – that is, identify with – ideas of racial difference that saw 'others' as inferior to white Europeans. Fanon explains that the 'black man' is made to believe in his inferiority to the 'white colonisers' through psychological aspects of colonisation, such as the imposition of the coloniser's language, culture, religion and education systems. Through such impositions, the colonised come to believe they are a culturally inferior other. This internalisation made it easier for colonisers to justify and maintain their rule. Postcolonialism thus brings into focus how racial binaries – that is, how races are constructed as different, opposite or 'other' – continue even after the end of formal colonial rule. It highlights how *racialised othering* frames not just history, but contemporary debates such as national security, nuclear politics, nationalism, culture, immigration, international aid and the struggle for indigenous rights.

An example of racialised othering can be found in discourses around nuclear non-proliferation. In such discourses, countries and their leaders in the Global

South are usually deemed not to be trusted with nuclear weapons. These dominant discourses construct these states as dangerous, unpredictable or unaccountable and as violating basic norms on human rights. One need only look at how North Korea and Iran, two states that have pursued nuclear proliferation, are portrayed as rogue states in US foreign policy discourse. Yet, for decades, the West's disregard for human rights may be seen in uranium mining that has often taken place on lands that are populated by indigenous peoples around the world – including in the United States – and has caused death, illness and environmental degradation. Most importantly, what is often missing from the nuclear debate is the fact that the United States is the only power to have ever used nuclear weapons (aside from testing), when it dropped atomic bombs on the Japanese cities of Nagasaki and Hiroshima in 1945, with horrific and devastating loss of life.

Therefore, for postcolonial scholars such as Shampa Biswas (2014), the notion that some states can be trusted with nuclear weapons while others cannot because they are less developed, less mature in their approach to human life or less rational is a racialised discourse. In debates such as these, postcolonialism asks not who can be trusted with such weapons, but rather *who determines who can be trusted – and why?* Simply looking at the competition between states to accrue nuclear weapons will not tell us enough about the workings of power in international relations – such as how a nuclear arms race is underpinned by the power of some states to construct other states so that they are deemed not capable of having any such weapons at all.

Postcolonialism and the marginalisation of women of colour

As with all theories of IR, there are internal debates among postcolonial scholars and in this case also a significant overlap with feminism – especially 'third wave' feminism that became prominent in the 1990s. bell hooks (2000) observed that the so-called 'second wave' of feminism of the mid- to late twentieth century had emerged from women in a position of privilege and did not represent African American women such as herself who remain on the margins of society, politics and the economy. She called for an alternative, critical and distinctive feminist activism and politics.

For example, does a black woman from a poor neighbourhood on Chicago's south side experience sexism in the same way as a white woman from its wealthier suburbs? Women who share the same ethnic identity might experience sexism in different ways because of their class. The same might be true for women of colour and white women from the same social class. Women of colour and white women in the United States experience 'heteropatriarchy' – a societal order marked by white male heterosexual domination – differently even if they come from the same social class. An illustration of how this works may be found in the video of Beyonce's 'Lemonade' which not only draws on how sexism is filtered through this patriarchal order but also explores how race, gender, class and sexuality are intimately intertwined in the history of black women.

The fact that some black women may be more privileged in relation to class may not take away from their experience of racism. For this reason (and others), feminist postcolonial scholars (see Chowdhry and Nair 2002) call for more attention to the intersections of race and/or ethnicity, nationality, class *and* gender. By doing so they address the ways that different aspects of one's identity, such as race, gender, class, sexuality and so forth, intersect to create multiple and distinct forms of oppression so that no one aspect can be privileged over another in understanding oppression. Instead, various identities must all be understood as intersecting in producing one's experience of oppression. This idea of 'intersectionality' is central to third-wave feminist approaches.

Postcolonial feminists share a desire to go beyond simply analysing the impacts of patriarchy, gender inequality and sexual exploitation. Instead, they highlight the need to fight not only patriarchy (broadly understood as the power of men over women) but also the classism and racism that privileges white women over women of colour. They question the idea of universal solidarity in women's movements, arguing that the struggle against patriarchy as well as social inequality must be situated in relation to racial, ethnic and sexual privilege. For example, while Western feminism has often portrayed the veil as a symbol of oppression of women, many Algerian women adopted the veil, standing alongside men, when protesting French rule. To them, it was a symbol of opposition to white, colonial patriarchy. In many other parts of the colonised world, women stood shoulder to shoulder with men in nationalist movements to overthrow colonial rule, showing that women in different cultural, social and political contexts experience oppression in very different ways. Postcolonial feminists are committed to an intersectional approach that uncovers the deeper implications of how and why systemic violence evident in war, conflict, terror, poverty, social inequality and so forth has taken root. Understanding power thus requires paying attention to these intersections and how they are embedded in the issue at hand.

Postcolonial feminism asserts that women of colour are triply oppressed due to their (1) race/ethnicity, (2) class status and (3) gender. An example can be found in the employment conditions of the many women in the Global South who work in factories producing textiles, semi-conductors, and sporting and consumer goods for export to the West. In one such factory in Thailand, the Kader Toy Factory, a fire in 1993 killed 220 female factory workers and seriously injured over 500 more. The doors to the building were locked at the time of the fire. The tragedy revealed the exploitation and deplorable working conditions of these women, who were employed by local contractors of American companies to make toys and stuffed animals for sale in Western markets. Despite decades of such abuses, there was little attention given to the conditions in these factories, or to the tragedy of the fire, in the mainstream Western media. One opinion piece captured the shocking disregard for these women's lives,

> These executives know that their profits come from the toil of the young and the wretched in the Far East; they can live with that – live well, in fact. But they do not want to talk about dead women and girls stacked in the factory yard like so much rubbish, their bodies eventually to be carted away like any other industrial debris (Herbert 1994).

In another tragedy, the Rana Plaza – a garment factory in Dhaka, Bangladesh – collapsed, killing 1,135 garment workers, mostly women. It threw a spotlight on the workings of the global garment industry. Popular Western clothing lines profit from low wages, exploitation and sweatshop conditions by producing their clothes in countries with lax building codes and regulations and non-existent (or inadequate) labour standards. The clothing lines do not then hold the factories to account for working conditions or safety. Postcolonial scholars argue that the deeply exploitative conditions and the disregard for the safety of these workers show that lesser value is ascribed to brown bodies compared to white ones.

While there was much more coverage of this industrial accident in the Western media and the brands whose clothing was being made at the Rana Plaza did suffer some momentary bad publicity, there has been little sustained effort to right the wrongs in the operations of multinational firms. The quest for the highest possible profit margins forces developing countries into a 'race to the bottom' in which they compete to have the cheapest labour and production costs in order to attract investment from multinational corporations.

The results are low wages, exploitation and low safety standards. Post-colonial scholarship explains the failure to change these conditions by exposing how race, class and gender come together to obscure the plight of these workers, meaning that the factory overseers, like the owners of the Rana Plaza and Kader operations, are not held accountable until tragedy strikes. Even when they are held accountable, the punishment does not extend to the Western corporations further up the chain who sub-contract the task of exploiting workers – and ultimately killing some of them in these cases. It is almost impossible to imagine that a tragedy of a similar scale in a Western state would prompt so little action against those responsible or allow the conditions that caused it to continue virtually unchecked.

Conclusion

Postcolonialism interrogates a world order dominated by major state actors and their domineering interests and ways of looking at the world. It challenges notions that have taken hold about the way states act or behave and what motivates them. It forces us to ask tough questions about how and why a hierarchical international order has emerged and it further challenges mainstream IR's core assumptions about concepts such as power and how it operates. Postcolonialism forces us to reckon with the everyday injustices and oppressions that can reveal themselves in the starkest terms through a particular moment of crisis. Whether it has to do with the threat of nuclear weapons or the deaths of workers in factories churning out goods for Western markets, postcolonialism asks us to analyse these issues from the perspectives of those who lack power. While postcolonialism shares some common ground with other critical theories in this regard, it also offers a distinctive approach. It brings together a deep concern with histories of colonialism and imperialism, how these are carried through to the present – and how inequalities and oppressions embedded in race, class and gender relations on a global scale matter for our understanding of international relations. By paying close attention to how these aspects of the global play out in specific contexts, postcolonialism gives us an important and alternative conceptual lens that provides us with a different set of theoretical tools to unpack the complexities of this world.

10

Towards a Global IR?

AMITAV ACHARYA

The study of International Relations is growing rapidly all over the world. IR students in Western universities are an increasingly multicultural lot, drawn from many different parts of the world. There is also a proliferation of IR departments and programmes in universities outside the West, especially in large countries such as China, India, Turkey, Brazil and Indonesia. However, IR is not yet a truly global discipline that captures the full range of ideas, approaches and experiences of both Western and non-Western societies. IR theories and concepts remain heavily biased in favour of Western Europe and the United States. Consequently, they neglect the experiences and relationships in other parts of the world, or offer a poor fit for understanding and explaining them.

The idea of a global IR challenges traditional IR's neglect and marginalisation of the voices and experiences of the non-Western world, or the Global South. The principal aim of global IR is to 'bring the Rest in'. It calls for greater participation from scholars from the Global South in the IR discipline and the broadening of the way IR is taught and written in the dominant centres of knowledge in the West. The purpose of global IR is to ensure the transformation of the discipline into something that actually captures and explains the relationships among states and societies in all parts of the world: East, West, North, South. A global IR perspective on IR theory does not seek to displace existing theories, but challenges them to broaden their horizons and acknowledge the place and role of the non-Western world.

The reasons for the hitherto Western dominance of IR are many. One is the hegemonic status of Western scholars, publications and institutions in IR and their widespread belief that the Western IR theory has discovered the right path to understanding IR, or the right answers to the puzzles and problems of the day. Compounding the problem is a serious lack of institutional resources in the non-Western world. Add to this the challenges facing scholars from non-English speaking countries in getting published in major IR journals or to pursue the major debates and developments in the field that are mainly carried out in the English language. Another factor is the close link between IR academics and governments in many developing countries (although this is also a feature in the West), which promotes policy-oriented research at the expense of theoretical work. There is also the tendency among many IR scholars in the Global South towards an uncritical acceptance of Western theory – and a resulting lack of confidence to take on Western theorists. In this situation, what passes as theory is mostly the application of Western theoretical concepts and models to the local context, rather than injecting indigenous ideas and insights from local practices to the main body of IR theory.

The discipline of International Relations, as often presented in its mainstream textbooks and the learning and training programmes of major institution teaching, is said to have nominally begun in the United Kingdom in 1919 when the first named department and professorship in international politics was created in Aberystwyth, Wales. But it really developed in the United States after the Second World War. It can hardly be a coincidence that these countries were the leading powers of the world before and after the Second World War. According to the traditional view, IR begins with the Peace of Westphalia (1648), when Europe developed the sovereign nation-state. This also coincided roughly with the rise of 'the West' via the European states system that expanded to the rest of the world due to European colonialism.

As non-Western nations became independent during the period of decolonisation post-1945, they inherited and adopted European ideas, institutions and practices. After the Second World War, while some European ideas retained their centrality, the United States added its own ideas and approaches. Europe before 1945 had managed international relations through a balance of power system, based on the idea that the stability of an international system is best ensured through an approximate parity among its major powers. Any attempt by any single power to become hegemonic (dominate the rest) should be defeated by an alliance among other powers in the system. The United States on the other hand sought to manage inter-national order through multilateral institutions, such as the United Nations and the International Monetary Fund. Although these institutions were theoretically open to participation by all nations, their purpose and agenda were heavily influenced by the interests and preferences of the United States and its allies.

Shaped by the ideas and practices of the West, the field of IR gave little attention to 'the Rest'. The traditional literature viewed non-Western countries as 'norm-takers' or 'passive subjects' – recipients of Western ideas and institutions – rather than active contributors to international order in their own right. Against this traditional view, Global IR offers an alternative narrative. IR as a discipline might have been invented in the West, but the substance of IR did not begin with the Peace of Westphalia in 1648, which marked the beginnings of the period of Western dominance. Other and older civilisations – such as India, China and Islam – pioneered different international systems and world orders. For this reason, their contribution should be more central to the study of IR. IR should study not only anarchic international systems like the Greek city-states system and Europe after the Peace of Westphalia, but also hierarchical systems such as prevailed in Asia and the Middle East before the advent of European colonialism.

Global IR also argues that international systems should be studied in terms of not only political-strategic interactions but also cultural and civilizational interactions. Many of the so-called modern concepts such as economic interdependence, balance of power, and collective management of security – which are often traced by traditional IR to European ideas and practices – actually have multiple points of origin, both within and outside of Europe. With such a broader scope, IR then offers more space to the history, culture, economic systems and interactions and contributions of non-Western civilizations and states. IR is best understood as the product of interactions and mutual learning between all civilisations and states, even though some have been more powerful than others at different stages in history.

Broadly stated, the idea of global IR revolves around six main dimensions (see Acharya 2014 and 2016).

First, global IR calls for a new understanding of universalism or universality. The dominant meaning of universalism in IR today is deeply influenced by the European Enlightenment. As Robert Cox (2002, 53) puts it, 'In the Enlightenment meaning, universal meant true for all time and space.' His conception of universalism may be called 'particularistic universalism', in the sense of one set of ideas from Europe applying to all of humankind. This conception of universalism had a dark side: the suppression of diversity and the justification of European imperialism – which was inspired by the belief that European ideas, institutions and practices are superior to those of others and hence deserve to be imposed over other societies through force and occupations. An alternative to particularistic universalism is pluralistic universalism. This recognises the diversity among nations, respects it and yet seeks to find the common ground among them. It views IR as a discipline with multiple and global foundations.

Second, global IR calls for IR to be more authentically grounded in world history, rather than Western history – and in the ideas, institutions, intellectual perspectives and practices of both Western and non-Western societies. 'Bringing the Rest in' does not mean simply using the non-Western world as a testing ground to revalidate existing IR theories after a few adjustments and extensions. Global IR must be a two-way process. A key challenge for theories and theorists of global IR is to develop concepts and approaches from non-Western contexts on their own terms, and apply them not only locally but also to other contexts, including the larger global canvas.

Third, global IR subsumes, rather than supplants existing IR knowledge, including the theories, methods and scientific claims that we are already familiar with. I fully recognise that IR theories are hardly monolithic or unchanging when it comes to dealing with the non-Western world. Some theories, especially postcolonialism and feminism, have been at the forefront of efforts to recognise events, issues, agents and interactions outside the West and drawing theoretical insights from them to enrich the study of IR. Realism is ahead of liberalism in drawing insights from the non-Western world. For example, realists recognise the thinking of India's Kautilya or China's legalist thinkers, such as Han Feizi, as forerunners of Machiavelli or Hobbes. Realism has also added new variants to its theoretical family that have rendered it more relevant to the non-Western world than in its classical forms. Constructivism has been especially important in opening space for scholarship on the non-Western world because of its stress on culture and identity. Realism and liberalism privilege material determinants of international relations, such as power or wealth. These are often in short supply in the developing world. But ideas and norms are not, and they are often the main mechanisms through which the developing countries make their contribution to international relations. Liberalism is also useful in this sense as it identifies and prescribes three major pathways to peace: economic interdependence, multilateral institutions and democracy. The world has seen increasing trends towards these in the developing world. Global economic interdependence has grown since the end of the Cold War. There has been growing regional economic interdependence in East Asia, a critical region of the world. Multilateral institutions have proliferated, including in relatively newer areas such as cyberspace and climate change. To a lesser degree, democratisation has taken hold in the developing world, especially in Latin America and parts of East Asia, such as Indonesia and Myanmar. These developments could potentially make liberalism more relevant to under-standing the international politics of the non-Western world.

At the same time, global IR does not leave the mainstream theories – realism, liberalism and constructivism – *as is*. Instead, it urges them to rethink their assumptions and broaden the scope of their investigation. For realism, the challenge is to look beyond conflicts induced by national interest and distribution of power and acknowledge other sources of agency, including culture, ideas and norms that make states and civilisations not clash, but embrace and learn from each other. For liberals, there is a similar challenge to look beyond American hegemony as the starting point of investigating multilateralism and regionalism and their institutional forms. Liberalism also needs to acknowledge the significant variations in cooperative behaviour that exist in different local contexts, as no single model of integration or interactions can account for all or most of them. For constructivism, taking stock of different forms of agency in the creation and diffusion of ideas and norms remains a major challenge.

Fourth, global IR gives centre stage to regions. Regionalism today is less state-centric and encompasses an ever-widening range of actors and issues. Regionalism is sometimes viewed as the antithesis of universalism, but the two can be complimentary. Groupings such as the European Union (EU), Association of Southeast Asian Nations (ASEAN), and the African Union (AU) actually compliment the role of the United Nations in peacekeeping, humanitarian operations and conflict management. The study of regions is not just about how regions self-organise their economic, political and cultural space – it is also about how they relate to each other to shape global order. In addition, focusing on regions is central to forging a close integration between disciplinary approaches (which often have a global scope) and area (or regional) studies.

Fifth, a truly global IR cannot be based on cultural exceptionalism and parochialism. Exceptionalism is the tendency to present the characteristics of a social group as homogenous, collectively unique and superior to those of others. Claims about exceptionalism are frequently associated with the political agendas and purposes of the ruling elite, as evident in concepts such as 'Asian Values' or 'Asian human rights' or 'Asian Democracy'. These are usually associated with variations of authoritarian rule because they originated in the 1990s from such countries as Lee Kuan Yew's Singapore, Mahathir Mohamad's Malaysia and Deng Xiaoping's China. Similarly, exceptionalism in IR often justifies the dominance of big powers over the weak. Before its defeat in the Second World War, Japan sought to establish an empire over Asia under the pretext of a distinctive pan-Asian culture and identity. Today, the rise of China has raised the possibility of an international system in Asia dominated by Chinese (Confucian) values and suzerain institutions, such as its historical tributary system.

Finally, global IR takes a broad conception of and multiple forms of agency. Not so long ago, agency in international relations was primarily viewed in terms of a 'standard of civilisation' in which the decisive element was the capacity of states to defend their sovereignty, wage war, negotiate treaties, enforce compliance and manage the balance of power. This self-serving, ahistorical and brazenly racist formulation by the European colonial powers ignored the fact that even the most sophisticated forms of statecraft were present in many early non-Western civilisations. While the mainstream IR theories viewed the so-called Third World or Global South as marginal to the games that nations play, some of the critical theories actually thrived on this presumed marginality. They rightly criticised mainstream theories for excluding the South but did little exploration of alternative forms of agency in the South. While global disparities in material power are not going to disappear, we need to adopt a broader view of agency in international relations, going beyond military power and wealth. Agency is both material as well as ideational. Agency is not the prerogative of the strong, but can manifest as the weapon of the weak. Agency can be exercised in global transnational space as well as at regional and local levels. Agency can take multiple forms. Agency means constructing new rules and institutions at the regional level either to challenge or to support and strengthen global order.

For example, China's nationalist leader before the Second World War, Sun Yat-sen, is the father of the idea of international development that came to underpin post-war institutions such as the World Bank. India's Jawaharlal Nehru was the first to propose a ban on nuclear testing. The Latin American countries adopted a declaration of human rights months before the Universal Declaration of Human Rights was drafted at the United Nations in New York. And Asian nations played an important role in the making of subsequent United Nations covenants on civil and politics rights and economic, social and cultural rights.

Agency means conceptualising and implementing new pathways to security, development and justice. In the 1960s, African countries developed formal and informal rules to maintain their postcolonial boundaries within the framework of the Organization of African Unity, which was later replaced by the African Union in 2000. Along with the African Union, a major role in the creation of the *'Responsibility to Protect'* (R2P) norm was played by African political leaders such as Nelson Mandela, diplomats such as Francis Deng (a Sudanese) and Mohamed Sahnoun (an Algerian) and the former United Nations Secretary-General, Kofi Annan. Indian economist Amartya Sen and Pakistani economist Mahbub ul Haq frontally challenged the orthodox Western model of development that focuses on national economic power and growth rates in Gross Domestic Product (GDP). They put forward the alternative and broader notion of *human development*, which focuses on enhancing individual capabilities through primary education and health. As is evident, some of these acts of agency are not just for specific regions or for the South itself, but are important to global governance as a whole. Using this broader framework of agency, global IR gives a central place to the voices and agency of the South, to Southern perspectives on global order and to the changing dynamics of North–South relations.

With the fundamentals of global IR now laid out it is important to recall Robert Cox, who warned that 'theory is always for someone and for some purpose' (1981, 129). Who is global IR for and for what purpose? Because global IR does not reject IR's existing theories, but seeks to accommodate them, it is open to criticism that it might end up preserving IR's basic structure – albeit filling in new contents by collecting concepts around the world. In other words, global IR might end up globalising traditional IR theories and concepts. There is also the risk of over-focusing on the stronger and more resource-rich non-Western countries at the expense of the weaker countries of the developing world. Another challenge for global IR is how to study all nations, civilisations and issue areas under one framework without obscuring the cultural, political and economic variations among them. Attempting this also carries the risk of making IR too broad, lessening its analytic value and making theory-building difficult. These risks are not trivial, but keeping them in focus would help scholars to positively advance a discipline that clearly requires a new, global, perspective.

Part Two

EXPANSION PACK

11

Green Theory

HUGH C. DYER

In the 1960s there was public recognition of the global environmental crisis arising from the 'tragedy of the commons', which is the idea that as self-interested individuals, humans will overuse shared resources such as land, fresh water and fish. In the 1970s the first United Nations conference on the subject was held and by the 1980s green political parties and public policies had emerged. This coincided with a demand for a green theory to help explain and understand these political issues. By the 1990s, International Relations had come to recognise the natural environment as an increasingly significant source of questions for the discipline, requiring theoretical as well as practical attention – especially in the wake of mounting evidence that human actions were significantly changing our global climate and presenting security problems as well as ecological ones.

The basics of green theory

Ecological thought addresses the interests of nature itself rather than only the interests of humanity in nature. Green theory captures this orientation in political terms of value and agency (Goodin 1992) – what is to be valued, by whom and how to get it. Green theory belongs to the critical theory tradition, in the sense that environmental issues evoke questions about relations between and among ourselves and others in the context of community and collective decision-making. In turn this has always raised the question of where the boundaries of political community are. For environmental problems, which transcend boundaries, these questions take the form of asking at what level of political community we should seek a solution. For green theorists, the answers are found in alternative ideas about political association based on our ecological relationships.

The introduction of environmental issues into IR has had some influence, but their theoretical significance and practical policy implications may be viewed either as compatible or as irreconcilable with traditional assumptions and current practices. If viewed traditionally, then environmental issues can simply be added to the list of issues dealt with by existing means, for existing ends. If viewed alternatively, then these issues may lead to theoretical and practical transformation. Because theory and practice are linked, when environmental issues challenge existing practice they also raise new questions that IR theory must contend with. The obvious practical challenges of environmental change have not yet transformed IR theory – or even practice very much. The continued prevalence of competitive state relations is not conducive to environmental cooperation or encouraging to green thought. However, there has been theoretical development and some practical progress and a wide-ranging literature has emerged viewing a variety of environmental issues from different theoretical perspectives. If this doesn't amount to a single clear vision, it certainly represents a longer-term view about humankind's common future.

Typically, environmental issues are buried in IR texts under other headings and with little acknowledgement of their unique theoretical significance. Environmentalism-themed scholarship is generally accepting of the existing framework of political, social and economic structures of world politics. While there are of course established forms of critical thought, these address relations within and between human communities, rather than human relations with the non-human environment. For example, liberalism empha-sises individual rights of choice and consumption but is not fundamentally concerned with the environmental consequences of that consumption. Consequently, most forms of environmentalism seek to establish theoretical positions and practical solutions through existing structures, or in line with existing critiques of such structures. If less critical in orientation, then these views are likely to be compatible with a liberal position in IR (viewing international cooperation as being of general benefit to states). If more critical in orientation, then environmentalism may align itself to a critique of the capit-alist world system (maldistribution of benefits to people), if not challenging its commitment to production and consumption per se. An environmentalist perspective, while identifying environmental change as an issue, attempts to find room for the environment among our existing categories of other concerns, rather than considering it to be definitional or transformational.

Those frustrated by the lack of recognition of the environmental challenge in international relations turned to the interdisciplinary science of ecology. Political ecology has allowed both an ecological perspective to inform political thought and a political understanding of our environmental circumstances. In particular, our circumstances have long been determined by a particular developmental path that depends on the over-consumption of natural resources. Specifically, our political-economic practices of production, distribution and consumption are intended to meet our immediate human needs and desires. However, these practices are reflected in a growth-dependent global market economy that is not designed to achieve environmental sustainability or recognise ecological limits. This economy has provided material development of a kind, but with such uneven benefits and widespread collateral damage – including to the environment – that it has not provided human development in an ecological context. From an ecological perspective, there has been a general criticism of development and even apparently progressive sustainable development practices. The well-known model of the 'tragedy of the commons' (Hardin 1968), in which our short-term, individual, rational choices destroy our environmental resources, has thus been applied to the planet as a whole. It is tragic because we can see it coming but seem unable or unwilling to do anything about it. That inability is more than a practical problem; it is a profound theoretical challenge. Hardin pointed out that such issues cannot be solved by technical means, but require a change in human values.

Moving beyond environmentalism and political ecology, green theory more radically challenges existing political, social and economic structures. In particular, it challenges mainstream liberal political and economic assumptions, including those extending beyond the boundaries of existing political communities (for conventional IR, this means states). Goodin (1992) suggests that a distinguishing feature of green theory is its reference to a coherent moral vision – a 'green theory of value' – which operates independently of a theory of practices or political agency. For example, a green morality might suggest that human material development should be curtailed in the interest of preserving non-human nature. This would limit our freedom to consume however much we can acquire. The need to put some limits on traditional liberties suggests an approach that puts nature before people. Green theory, in this sense, is ecocentric.

Ecocentrism (ecology-centred thought) stands against anthropocentrism (human-centred thought). This is not because ecocentrism ignores human needs and desires, but rather because it includes those within a wider ecological perspective. Ecocentrism prioritises healthy ecosystems because they are a prerequisite to human health and wellbeing. In contrast, anthropocentrism sees only the short-term instrumental value of nature to humans. This ecocentric/anthropocentric distinction is at the heart of green theory. The holistic ecocentric perspective implies a rejection of the split between domestic and international politics, given that arbitrary boundaries between nations do not coincide with ecosystems. For example, air and water pollution can cross a border and climate change cuts across all borders and populations. Simply, human populations are ecologically interconnected. This impacts on how we understand and deal with transboundary and global environmental issues collectively, setting aside national self-interest.

The traditional IR concern with the state, in an international system of states, is a challenge to thinking about environmental issues. As a central feature of the historical Westphalian model of sovereign (self-determining) nation-states, the concept of sovereignty (ultimate authority) has been particularly troubling. Sovereignty neither describes the modern reality of political control nor offers a reliable basis for human identity or wellbeing. Global environmental problems require global solutions. This requires that we develop our under-standing of the 'global' as an alternative organising principle and perhaps look to green social movements rather than states for theoretical insights. This gives rise to the question of whether we need to give up on the idea of countries with borders as still being relevant to people's lives, or recast them in some more ecologically appropriate way with reference to how people live in relation to their environment. This will likely entail a more global than local kind of ethics. In part this hinges on our view of the need for political structures (big government, small government or no government) and the level or extent of their development. For example, we could promote centralised global political structures, such as an institution for governing environmental issues (Biermann 2001), or allow a variety of decentralised, even anarchical, interconnected local structures to emerge as circumstances require (Dyer 2014).

Decentralisation, or the transfer of authority and decision-making from central to local bodies, has certain attractive features, such as self-determination and democratic accountability. Ecologically there seem to be advantages as well, since small communities may depend more on immediate local resources and so be more likely to care for their environment. Local communities are more likely to conceive of the natural environment and their relationship to it in less instrumental terms, viewing it more as their home, thus addressing one of the key reasons for the environmental crisis.

For example, the concept of 'bioregionalism', where human society is organised within ecological rather than political boundaries, raises intriguing issues of knowledge, science, history, culture, space and place in an ecological context (McGinnis 1999). For instance, our sense of identity might derive more from familiar environmental surroundings than from the idea of nationality, such that we have greater inherited knowledge and understanding of our local environment than of our political location. However, there are also a number of objections to decentralisation, or greater localisation of decision-making. These include the concern that it would not promote cross-community cooperation as it is too parochial (too exclusively local; the problem of nationalism), and this would mean little chance of developing effective mechanisms to deal with global problems. In effect, it might just reproduce a troublesome sovereign-state model of politics on a smaller scale.

To date IR theory has shown concern with transformations in our political communities but somewhat less concern with transformations in our ecological communities. Perhaps this is because we are not yet sure how a cosmopolitan global sense of community colours our local relationships.

Green theory and climate change

Climate change is the dominant environmental issue of our age, caused by our dangerous reliance on fossil fuels. Green theory helps us to understand this in terms of long-term ecological values rather than short-term human interests. These interests are generally pursued by states through investments in technology, but there is no easy technical solution to human-induced climate change. From the perspective of green theory, this technical impasse requires a change in human values and behaviour and therefore presents an opportunity for political innovation or even a transformative shift in global politics. IR theory can explain why climate change is a difficult problem for states to solve because of economic competition and disincentives to cooperation. However, it cannot provide an alternative framework to explain how this might be addressed. IR remains overly focused on states and their national interests rather than other actors that may be more cooperative, such as cities and communities or non-governmental organisations and green social movements.

A green theory perspective on climate change understands it as a direct consequence of human collective choices. Specifically, these choices have led to historically anthropocentric economic practices of historically arbitrary political groups (states), who have exploited nature in their own short-term interests. Climate change presents a clear case of injustice to both present and future humans who are not responsible for causing it and to the ecosystem as a whole. Therefore, a solution requires an ecocentric theory of value and a more ethical than instrumental attitude to human relations in our common future. Green theory helps us to redefine issues such as climate change in terms of long-term ecological values rather than short-term political interests.

At the international level efforts have been underway since before the 1992 United Nations Conference on Environment and Development in Rio, which gave rise to the UN Framework Convention on Climate Change (UNFCCC) and other environmental agreements. As with many issues caught up in the direct tension between environmental goals and developmental goals, any bargains struck are inadequate compromises.

For green theory there is no such tension in an ecological path to development, even if that path seems more costly in the short term. This is not least because some countries have developing still to do and hold already developed countries historically responsible for climate change – and no national actor is willing to bear global costs. After faltering efforts to address climate change through the terms of the UNFCCC's Kyoto Protocol, an outline agreement was eventually achieved in the Paris Accords of December 2015. Whether or not this effort will actually address the sources and consequences of climate change remains to be seen, but green theory suggests that a focus on human values and choices in communities is better than a focus on bargaining between states.

In a world of states with primary responsibilities to their own citizens, finding acceptable trade-offs between immediate economic wellbeing and longer-term ecological wellbeing is difficult. There is some prospect of powerful states (like China) or groups of states (like the European Union) leading the way and altering the structural parameters. However, the common ground available from an IR perspective of competing states is unlikely to be anywhere near the common ground envisioned by green theory. More fundamentally, it is unlikely to meet the challenge of climate change. Even with some political agreement, there remain significant differences about responsibility for historic climate change and the costs of adapting to an already changing climate that is affecting the least developed populations hardest. While it is possible for states to cooperate in order to make helpful environmental commitments, this is not directly related to action or change.

In any case, while international agreements are formally implemented by governments and other constitutional bodies, the key agents of change are a much wider range of non-state actors, smaller groups and individuals, which may suggest a kind of anarchy rather than hierarchy. In sum, a green solution to climate change could involve global governance institutions and communities working together – largely bypassing the state – in order to reduce damaging emissions, protect the climate and preserve the planetary ecology on which humans depend.

Green theory equips us with a new vantage point for analysing these developments. It also allows a broader ecological perspective on our common human interests and emphasises choices made within the ecological boundaries of climate change, rather than the political boundaries of economic advantage.

Conclusion

For IR, the contribution of green theory helps us re-examine the relationship between the state, the economy and the environment. IR normally sets this in the context of globalisation viewed from the limited perspective of states and markets – but globalisation also involves opportunities for developing shared global ecological values. Green theory has the potential to radically challenge the idea of sovereign nation states operating in competition and is thus part of the post-Westphalian trend in IR thought. Of course, the greater contribution of green theory, or its capacity for critical engagement with IR, lies in its very different origins – taking planetary ecology as a starting point and looking beyond our current political-economic structures. Green theory is thus able to offer not just an alternative description of our world but also a different logic for understanding it – and how we might act to change it. IR theory is likely to be disrupted and re-oriented by green theory, not so much because greens will win the arguments but because IR theorists will inevitably have to provide a coherent account of how we all live sustainably on our planet. This means that at some point we may have to stop theorising about the state-centric 'inter-national' and find another political point of reference in human relationships, such as policy networks or social movements.

12

Global Justice

ALIX DIETZEL

Global justice is a theory that exists within the broader school of cosmo-politanism, which focuses on the importance of the individual as opposed to the state, community or culture. Cosmopolitans take the individual as their starting point because they believe that all human beings have equal moral worth and therefore have the right to equal moral consideration. In this sense, even if cosmopolitans disagree on how to ensure that individuals are the subject of equal moral concern, the focus of these differing approaches is the value of the individual. This focus on the moral importance of the individual has led some cosmopolitan scholars to critically engage with theories of justice, which are traditionally confined to the state and contained within the realm of political (not international) theory. This endeavour has led to the theory of global justice, which seeks to investigate the question of how best to secure a just life for all individuals on Planet Earth, regardless of their nationality or status.

The basics of global justice

Justice, at its core, concerns itself with who deserves what and why. True to their cosmopolitan roots, contemporary global justice scholars concern them-selves with the moral worth of the individual, regardless of place of birth, and focus on problems of global cohabitation in which individuals are not yet treated as morally equal or where the moral focus has traditionally been on states. To engage with such problems, global justice scholars usually focus on what individuals across the world deserve and how distribution of these entitlements can be achieved. The answers to these types of questions vary significantly depending on which problem is being addressed.

John Rawls' (1971) *Theory of Justice* set out a theory that political structures (typically states) can determine who deserves what and why due to the power to make laws, raise taxes and dispense public spending. Therefore, such structures should be built carefully to ensure a just distribution of rights and duties between all citizens. Hence, Rawls' idea was one of *distributive justice*. Rawls was not advocating for communism, where all wealth is shared equally, but for a society where inequality was moderated so that those who were disadvantaged (for whatever reason) were at least able to live a decent life. Rawls theorised that such a structure could only exist within a democratic society, or in other words, a specific type of state. Therefore, Rawls' account of justice describes the potential for a just human existence for those fortunate enough to live within such a state – but his theory was not designed to apply internationally as no such formal structure of global distributive justice exists.

Cosmopolitan scholars take issue with Rawls' state-centric approach to justice and argue that questions of justice must include all humans, regardless of state association. For example, Charles Beitz (1975) argues that limiting questions of justice to the national level in the modern global era is morally inappropriate, because we now have global institutions that may be able to perform some of the basic functions of the state, such as collect forms of taxation or make laws. Thomas Pogge (1989) stresses that global inequalities between individuals call for a global approach to justice that can effectively respond to these inequalities. Although these scholars ground their arguments in different ways, they both advocate for a widening of the scope of justice to the global level. These types of arguments are where the term 'global justice' originates and provide the bedrock for its emergence as a theory of IR.

When discussing global poverty, Thomas Pogge (2001) and Gillian Brock (2010) argue that poverty alleviation should focus on redistributing wealth and resources between rich and poor individuals. When analysing humanitarian intervention, scholars such as Mary Kaldor (2010) and Daniele Archibugi (2004) make the case that individuals must be prioritised over state-centric non-intervention laws. Furthermore, scholars such as Garrett Brown (2012) analyse the issue of global health and argue that the health of individuals is determined by global structures to make the case for reform. Contemporary global justice scholars focus on problems as diverse as gender inequality, immigration and refugees, warfare and climate change. This implies that the question of who deserves what, and why, covers a wide range of topics, most of which are contemporary international relations problems. This is why the discipline of global justice is so relevant to IR, because global justice scholars concern themselves with analysing and assessing fundamental problems caused by global cohabitation. In this sense, it is a modern theory that will continue to be relevant as long as global problems exist.

Although global justice scholars usually assert that individuals must be the central unit of moral concern when exploring global problems, it is important to note that these scholars often prioritise different goals in order to ensure that individuals are the subject of equal moral concern. For example, some scholars emphasise human rights, some discuss the importance of institutions operating fairly (referred to as procedural justice), some emphasise the importance of human capability, while others are concerned with fair global social processes. It is important to keep this diversity in mind when studying global justice. No two scholars have the exact same aims, which implies a healthy diversity of ideas within the field. This is true even within more narrow subjects, such as climate justice, where authors have many different ideas on how to achieve a just response to the problem of climate change.

While you might assume that an approach that seeks to treat all humans on Earth better is popular, or logical, global justice also attracts some notable criticisms. David Miller (2007) argues that national borders are more important than cosmopolitan global justice. Miller believes that coming to an agreement on principles of justice requires a common history and culture and that defining global principles is not possible because of national differences on conceptions of what is 'good' or 'right'. Thomas Nagel (2005) and Michael Blake (2001) both argue that global justice cannot be achieved without the backing of powerful global institutions. However, global institutions that have power over individuals and states simply do not exist (yet), rendering discussions about global principles of justice futile. Finally, Iris Marion Young (2011) regards cosmopolitanism as a Western-centric theory that does not have the global appeal it purports to have. After all, global justice is based on the importance of the individual and often makes appeal to human rights and other liberal norms, which some perceive as Western ideals, not universal ones. These criticisms do not take away from the importance of global justice: like all theories of IR, its theoretical development is spurred on by answering its critics.

Global justice and climate change

Climate change requires actors from around the world to come together and agree on how to move forward. As temperatures continue to rise and the global response lags behind what scientists recommend, global justice scholars are becoming increasingly interested in climate change and its global (mis)management. Spurred on by the global nature of the problem and the injustices it presents, global justice scholars have also turned their attention to climate change for several important reasons.

First, climate change is undoubtedly a global problem and global justice scholars are keen to engage with such problems. Greenhouse gas emissions cannot be confined within a state, they rise into the atmosphere and cause global temperature changes within and outside of their original state borders. Although it is difficult to establish direct blame or fault, it is nonetheless undeniable that virtually all individuals, states and corporations contribute to some degree to climate change. In this sense, the global nature of the climate change problem defies conventional assumptions about state sovereignty and justice, which is what makes it so interesting to global justice scholars.

Second, climate change requires a global solution, which suits global justice scholars who are interested in providing recommendations for problems of global cohabitation. No one state can stop climate change on its own. There is no doubt that combatting climate change will require a collaborative effort, implying the need for global agreements. Coming to such agreements will inevitably involve discussion about which actors must lower emissions and by how much or even which actors should contribute to the costs of climate change – such as helping certain populations adapt to rising sea levels or extreme weather. These are, by their nature, questions of distributive justice and are therefore of interest to global justice scholars.

Third, climate change presents an unfair distribution of benefits and burdens between morally equal individuals, who are the key concern of global justice scholars. Climate change will most negatively affect those living in less developed countries who have done the least to contribute to the causes of climate change, while those living in developed countries, who have contributed the most emissions, will likely suffer the least. This is because less developed countries are more often located in areas which will bear the brunt of the problems associated with climate change. Furthermore, developing states typically do not have as many resources as developed states to adapt to dangerous weather patterns. For example, the Solomon Islands has already lost five small islands as a result of climate change and yet it is one of the lowest emitting countries in the world. Paul Harris (2010, 37) argues that the climate change problem 'cries out for justice' because the effects of climate change fall disproportionately on people who are already vulnerable, cannot adequately protect themselves and have not significantly contributed to the problem.

Although global justice scholars agree that climate change will affect individuals and are therefore concerned with addressing the problem, these scholars have different ideas on what exactly is at stake and what should therefore be prioritised. For example, Simon Caney (2010) defines three distinct rights that are predicted to be threatened by climate change: the right to life, the right to food and the right to health – and any programme combating climate change should not violate these.

Tim Hayward (2007) defines a right specific to the climate change problem: ecological space – a human right to live in an environment free of harmful pollution adequate for health and wellbeing. Hayward's approach differs from Caney's because his priority is not protecting human rights that already exist in international law but rather creating new climate related rights that must be defended.

Patrick Hayden's (2010) conception of rights encompasses both environment specific substantive and procedural rights. Hayden's substantive rights include the right to be protected from environmental harm and his procedural rights include the right to be fully informed about the potential effects of environmental hazards, the right to participate in democratic procedures for climate policymaking and the right to complain about existing conditions, standards and policies (Hayden 2010, 361–362). In this sense, Hayden is concerned not merely with basic rights but also with fair procedures.

The debate about rights is important because defining who deserves what can help guide a discussion on what should be done about climate change and who should be responsible for climate change action. For example, if the right to health must be protected, this could imply that lowering emissions is not enough and that populations must be protected from disease in other ways – for example, by inoculating vulnerable people against certain diseases or providing clean drinking water in drought-prone areas.

The question of who is responsible for climate change action is another key point of discussion amongst global justice scholars. The discipline of IR is traditionally concerned with relationships between states. Some scholars following this tradition and these debates usually focus on which states should contribute how much to climate change action.

Henry Shue (2014) advocates for the *Polluter Pays Principle*, which is based on examining who caused the problem to determine who should pay (and how much) for climate change action – and the *Ability to Pay Approach*, which asserts that the responsibility should be borne by the wealthy. Thomas Risse (2008) takes issue with these approaches and advocates for an index that measures per capita wealth and per capita emission rates, then groups countries into categories.

In this sense, the debate concerns how responsibility for climate change should be allocated, which is important for international relations as it reflects ongoing discussions between states, most recently when putting together the 2015 Paris Agreement. Other scholars are keen to include non-state actors in their conceptions of climate justice and responsibility.

Paul Harris points out that cosmopolitanism is traditionally concerned not only with states but also with individuals. For this reason he studies how individuals are affecting climate change and discovers that it is rich individuals who produce the most greenhouse gases, regardless of which state they live in. As he puts it, 'affluence is the primary and disproportionate cause of global environmental degradation' (Harris 2010, 130). These individuals have responsibility to act on climate change by (for example) travelling less, reducing meat consumption and buying fewer luxury items. Simon Caney (2010) argues that all agents (not just the wealthy) who contribute to emissions and have the means of lowering these, including individuals, states, corporations, sub-state political authorities and international financial institutions, should be held accountable.

These debates about the climate responsibilities of non-state actors are important to IR theory, which is traditionally concerned with how states relate to one another. By discussing which other actors might be responsible for climate change, global justice scholars are able to move the discipline of International Relations in a new direction.

Conclusion

International relations theory has traditionally been overly concerned with global (dis)order. Global justice scholars have contributed to widening the scope of IR theory by shifting the focus to individuals, on a planetary scale, and thereby approaching problems of global cohabitation in a new way. Yet despite signs of progress in academia, states seem to be more focused on managing conflict, distrust and disorder than on reaching global agreements and treating one another fairly. For that reason, global justice as an issue has been underrepresented in policy and global justice scholarship has not yet reached the same prominence as mainstream IR theories such as realism or liberalism. Nevertheless, in times of transnational terrorism, rising global inequalities, migration crises, pandemic disease and climate change – considerations of global cooperation, fairness and justice are more important than ever.

13

Queer Theory

MARKUS THIEL

Queer theory offers a significant avenue through which to deconstruct and then reconstruct established IR concepts and theories. Stemming from various fields that transcend a narrow view of IR, queer research applies an interdisciplinary outlook to advance new critical perspectives on sexualities, gender and beyond. A single viewpoint in a field as diverse as IR would unnecessarily limit the range of scholarly viewpoints. It would also preclude a nuanced debate about the contents and forms of lesbian, gay, bisexual and transgender (LGBT) perspectives, queer scholarship and queer scholarly politics in IR. Due to these themes, and because of its diversity, it is difficult to define queer theory precisely. Indeed, a narrow definition of it would not be in line with queer theoretical tenets. Queer theory is not just confined to sexualities or sexual rights. It also questions established social, economic and political power relations – and critically interrogates notions of security.

The basics of queer theory

Queer theory's origins are in LGBT studies – which focus on sexuality and gender. It soon distanced itself from those approaches due to disagreements with the stable identities that LGBT studies suggest. Queer theory emphasises the fluid and humanly performed nature of sexuality – or better, sexualities. It questions socially established norms and dualistic categories with a special focus on challenging sexual (heterosexual/homosexual), gender (male/female), class (rich/poor), racial (white/non-white) classifications. It goes beyond these so-called 'binaries' to contest general political (private/public) as well as international binary orders (democratic/authoritarian). These are viewed as over-generalising theoretical constructs that produce an either/or mode of analysis that hides more than it clarifies and is unable to detect nuanced differences and contradictions. But queer theory also analyses and critiques societal and political norms in particular as they relate to the experience of sexuality and gender. These are not viewed as private affairs. Just as feminists perceive of gender as a socially constructed public and political affair, so queer theorists argue with regards to sexuality and gender expression.

As the word 'queer' was used to describe homosexuals in the nineteenth century, queer theory traces its lineage from the study of sexuality in its private and public forms. A commonplace meaning attributed to the term revolves around being non-conforming in terms of sexuality and gender, thus adding an ambiguous notion to being or acting queer. Hence a queer approach towards sexual equality complicates identity-based LGBT advocacy, as queer thinking expresses a more challenging, fluid perspective. This split has become even more pronounced as the international politics of sexual orientation and gender identity receives an ever-increasing degree of public attention. Some states have implemented substantial equality provisions in order to prove that they are 'modern' or 'Western' enough, while others have responded with pushback in the form of homophobic legislation and persecution. Sexual orientation and gender identity rights, which themselves are questioned by queer theorists as overly reliant on Western liberal norms of human rights and democracy, have become points of political contention, eliciting domestic culture wars as well.

Consider the debate in the United States over whether transgender individuals should be free to use the toilet of their personal choice. The status of sexuality and gender politics in IR has clearly been elevated via cases such as this which can quickly transcend domestic politics and enter the international realm. In addition, it has also impacted apparently unrelated policies such as defence policies, health care and labour market regulations and thus created new avenues for the re-construction of conventional IR concepts. As a result, new perspectives are needed to explain this inherent part of the social and political world. Queer theory does not assume a uniform access to reality, but rather acknowledges that subjective knowledge(s) about sexuality, gender and other social aspects are constructed rather than pre-existent, fluid rather than stable, and not always in line with societal norms. In this sense, queer theory has moved beyond focusing simply on the experience of sexuality and gender.

Sexuality politics and the queer scholarship connected to it arrived late on the theoretical scene in part because sexuality and gender initially were anchored in the private, rather than the public, spheres. Scholars advanced critical and feminist viewpoints emerging from the writings of Michel Foucault (1976), Judith Butler (1990) and Eve Kosofsky Sedgwick (1990) among others. Foucault's groundbreaking linking of sexuality and knowledge to political power, and Butler's rejection of stable sexual orientation and gender identities in favour of everyday performed ones remain foundational notions. Kosofsky Sedgwick's calling attention to the discursive definition of homo/heterosexuality in society further defined queer thinking. These scholarly statements were hardly accepted in mainstream political science because they rejected objectivity and highlighted the conditional and unstable human nature of social and political orders, including IR questions of security and governance. Hence queer theory evolved largely in literature, philosophy, sociology and queer studies programmes without making substantial inroads into IR theorising.

Despite the distinct emergence of queer theory from these wider origins, some questions remain. One of the major issues is to what extent 'queer' should be adopted as a label for transgressive (socially unacceptable) forms of thinking and acting – as this would in turn create a queer/mainstream binary. This is something that queer scholars argue against. Another issue lies in the vague definition of queer theoretical tenets and terms, leading to uncertainty about how a queer theoretical lens can best be deployed in various disciplines by a wide range of individuals. In its application to IR, queer theory challenges many assumptions about world politics unrelated to sexuality and gender. It aims to deconstruct established simplistic binaries – such as insecurity/security or war/peace – and recognises the inherent instability of political and social orders. Instead, it embraces the fluid, performative and ambiguous aspects of world politics. Hence, it criticises those approaches to politics and society that assume natural and moral hierarchies. It problematises, for instance, the way in which non-traditional sexualities have become normalised according to 'hetero-normative' standards, including the aspiration towards marriage and child rearing. Queer theorists argue that this results in a societal integration of sexual minorities into mainstream consumer society – making them less willing (or able) to contest deeper political inequalities.

Queer theory perceives sexuality and gender as social constructs that shape the way sexual orientation and gender identity are displayed in public – and thereby often reduced to black-and-white issues that can be manipulated or distorted. With regard to more classical IR topics, it critically assesses the assumption that all societies find themselves at different points along a linear path of political and economic development or adhere to a universal set of norms. Hence it embraces ambiguity, failure and conflict as a counterpoint to a dominant progressive thinking evident in many foreign or development policies. As a scholarly undertaking, queer theory research constitutes of 'any form of research positioned within conceptual frameworks that highlight the instability of taken-for-granted meanings and resulting power relations' (Nash and Browne 2012, 4).

Weber (2014) highlights a lack of attention to queer theory by decrying the closed-mindedness of standard IR theories, arguing that queer scholarship in IR exists but is not recognised. The invisibility of queer theory is slowly changing, with case-study work on state homophobia (Weiss and Bosia 2013) or collective identity politics (Ayoub and Paternotte 2014) and the increasing relevance of transnational LGBT rights discourses for IR scholarship. But if empirical work in this area concentrates mainly on the agency of groups in their surrounding political structure, what is 'queer' about LGBT advocacy perspectives? These works offer comparative case studies from regional, cultural and theoretical peripheries to identify new ways of theorising the political subject by questioning the role of the state as we have come to accept it. They add to IR by broadening the knowledge about previously under-recognised perspectives that critically examine IR's apparently obvious core concepts (or 'myths', as Weber calls them) such as sovereignty, power, security and nationalism. They do so from the vantage point of the outsider and infuse these well-worn IR concepts with critical considerations and interpretations. Importantly, they contest existing dualistic binaries in mainstream IR – such as state/system, modern liberalism/premodern homophobia, and West/Rest. Queer IR scholars look for the contribution queer analysis can provide for re-imagining the political individual, as well as the international structure in which people are embedded.

Reflecting on the possible futures of queer theory, there are various important aspects to consider. Progress in LGBT politics is mainly limited to the Global West and North and evokes culture wars about how hetero-normative such advocacy should be. And, it elicits international (homo)colonialist contentions about the culturally intrusive manner by which LGBT rights are promoted. This becomes clear when powerful transnational groups, governments or international organisations propose to make foreign aid disbursement conditional on equality reforms in certain countries. At the same time, they do not sufficiently recognise that their explicit LGBT support increases the marginalisation of minorities in certain states. It has to be mentioned though, that many LGBT organisations have a better understanding of local contexts and often act with the cooperation of local activists, though typically in a weaker position than the intergovernmental institutions they are allied with. LGBT politics and queer IR research can inspire and parallel each other as long as sexual advocacy politics does not fall prey to overly liberal, patronising politics. No matter if in the domestic or international arenas a number of problematic issues remain with the alleged progress of LGBT politics: if predominantly gay and lesbian rights such as marriage and adoption equality are aimed for, can one speak of true equality while transgender individuals still lack healthcare access or protection from hate crimes? And if the normalisation of Western LGBT individuals into consuming, depoliticised populations leads to a weakening of solidarity with foreign LGBT activists and appreciation of their difference, what effects does this have on global LGBT emancipation? Queer theory is an important tool for helping to better appreciate the complexity of these debates.

Queer theory and sexual equality in Europe

Globalisation has equipped queer theorists and activists with an expanded terrain for intervention. With reference to LGBT advocacy politics, the emergence of numerous Western-organised non-governmental organisations but also local LGBT movements with the significant publicity they generate – be it positive or negative – expands transnational politics to a previously unknown degree. Both chip away at the centrality of the state in regulating and protecting its citizens. A key place this can be detected is within debates in the European Union (EU), which is an international organisation with supranational (law-making) powers over its member states.

The inclusion of LGBT individuals not as abject minorities but as human rights carriers with inherent dignity and individual rights of expression may transform the relationship between a marginalised citizenry and governmental authority – both at the state and EU level. But queer theory does not always align comfortably with the predominant political strategies advanced through transnational LGBT rights advocacy in Europe. It disputes many existing socio-political institutions such as neoliberal capitalism or regulatory citizenship that form the bedrocks of European politics. LGBT advocacy is, at times, viewed by queer theory as conforming, heteronormative, stereotyping and even (homo)nationalistic in its particular value-laden Western overtones. This is because it assumes that striving for Western standards of equality and inclusion is universally applicable and leads to liberation and inclusion. These become evident in the pressuring of more conservative European states to adopt certain policies, which often produce counter-productive tensions and expose vulnerable minorities. LGBT advocacy is aimed at inclusion within existing forms of representation rather than the appreciation of difference that queer theory strives at. Thus, LGBT organisations often appear 'de-queered' for political purposes to gain approval by the rest of society, which often leads to internal debates about their representation and goals.

Tensions between mainstream advocacy and radical queer approaches signify the need to rethink simplistic IR analytical approaches. Political tensions in the 'real' world prompt the queer IR theorist to question generally accepted, established conceptions of international governance. In doing so, queer theorists use existing literature or audio-visual material such as movies or even performances to go beyond the apparently obvious to deconstruct and then reconstruct IR events and processes. They often exhibit a critical perspective towards naturally assumed conditions of space and time that tend to conceal and flatten differences among actors and interpretations of international events. For example, Cynthia Weber (2016) uses Hillary Clinton's sexual rights speech at the United Nations in 2011 and contrasts it with Conchita Wurst's winning performance at the Eurovision song contest in 2014 to highlight a 'queer logic of statecraft' that contests traditional, gendered and binary approaches to governance. Weber highlights how despite transforming the notion of the homosexual from deviant into normal rights-holder in her speech, Clinton still produced an international binary of progressive versus intolerant states. On the other hand, Conchita Wurst – a character created by Thomas Neuwirth – challenged accepted notions of what is considered normal or perverse by performing in drag with a beard. In the course of this, Wurst destabilised racial, sexual, gendered and geo-political notions of what it means to be a European. Taken together, both cases show how seemingly stable ideas in international relations are far from natural. Instead, they are intentionally created, normalised, challenged and reconfigured.

Looking deeper at issues within Europe, the EU's justification of sexual non-discrimination on neoliberal market policies highlights the ambiguous positioning of the EU when it advocates limited equality provisions (Thiel 2015). This anti-discrimination policy is being implemented in the EU's complex multi-level governance system that includes EU institutions as rights 'givers', member states as not always compliant 'takers', and LGBT groups somewhere in the middle. In addition to this potentially problematic setting, the EU's anti-discrimination policy package applies only to employment-related discrimination. But Europe's largest LGBT advocacy group, the International Lesbian, Gay, Trans, Bisexual and Intersex Association (ILGA Europe), together with many other groups has been pressing the case for a broader anti-discrimination law covering all areas of life. This is complicated by the fact that a few powerful states do not want to broaden the existing market-based law and by EU hesitancy to reach beyond its focus on economic rights and freedoms.

It becomes evident that the dominance of neoliberalism as the EU's main rationale limits the rights attainment of LGBT individuals because it restricts alternative critical views. Given the EU's orientation, non-governmental organisations are pressured to prioritise market-principles such as labour participation, while becoming more dependent on governmental or EU funding. At the same time, this increase in non-governmental advocacy coin-cides with a retreat of governments in social and welfare sectors. This diminishes the potential for contesting existing policies and potentially their legitimacy, as groups have to link anti-discrimination activities with more societal and labour market inclusion if they want to retain funding from the

EU. Such reorientation around neoliberal EU objectives produces a hierarchy of rights which risks putting social inclusion and a wider sense of equality at the bottom.

This case study thus questions the cooperation of non-governmental advocacy organisations with a supranational governance system that is at least partly responsible for constraining national welfare policies. Moreover, the EU's valuation of rights is problematic because inalienable rights are being made an object of economic value and output. Yet it cannot be criticised in a system in which EU policy planning is protected by its supposed non-political regulatory, expert-led nature – reminding us of Foucault's knowledge–power linkage. It also implies that a reflection of norms is needed, in the way neoliberal heteronormativity is desired by political actors in the EU policy process and accordingly (re)produced or challenged by gender/sex-based rights groups. The feminist contribution to IR highlights uneven gendered power relations, but a critical political economy perspective that merges concerns about structural injustice with the thoughtful critique of queer theory's view on civil society inclusion adds profound insights into the politics of sexual rights recognition. This is most relevant here when considering queer theory's theoretical tenets such as taking seriously the distinct positions of political actors and the often troubling content of public policy.

Conclusion

The development of queer theory in IR suggests that more rigorous questions of the impact of LGBT issues in international politics have begun to be successfully answered. It highlights the valuable contribution to analysing IR through until now unrecognised perspectives on sexual and gender expression. Queer theory has also proven to be theoretically inclusive in ways that LGBT and feminist scholarship sometimes has not. A question that remains is whether queer theorists can recognise – and perhaps transcend – their own racial, class and Western-centric orientations. Such broadening would also make it easier to find common cause with other affected minorities – not least to move from a purely critical or deconstructive mode to a more transformative and productive one. Precisely because queer theory is able to transcend the focus on sexuality and gender through general analytical principles, it lends itself to interrogating a wide range of IR phenomena. In a time when IR is often accused of being parochial, queer theory is a necessary corrective to powerful myths and narratives of international orders.

14

Securitisation Theory

CLARA EROUKHMANOFF

Securitisation theory shows us that national security policy is not a natural given, but carefully designated by politicians and decision-makers. According to securitisation theory, political issues are constituted as extreme security issues to be dealt with urgently when they have been labelled as 'dangerous', 'menacing', 'threatening', 'alarming' and so on by a 'securitising actor' who has the social and institutional power to move the issue 'beyond politics'. So, security issues are not simply 'out there' but rather must be articulated as problems by securitising actors. Calling immigration a 'threat to national security', for instance, shifts immigration from a low priority political concern to a high priority issue that requires action, such as securing borders. Securitisation theory challenges traditional approaches to security in IR and asserts that issues are not essentially threatening in themselves; rather, it is by referring to them as 'security' issues that they become security problems.

The basics of securitisation theory

The end of the Cold War sparked a debate over ideas of security in IR between 'narrowers' and 'wideners'. The narrowers were concerned with the security of the state and often focused on analysing the military and political stability between the United States and the Soviet Union. Dissatisfied with this, wideners sought to include other types of threat that were not military in nature and that affected people rather than states. This expanded the security agenda by including concepts such as human security and regional security – together with ideas of culture and identity. Feminism had an important role in widening the agenda by challenging the idea that the sole provider of security was the state and that gender was irrelevant in the production of security. On the contrary, the state was often the cause of insecurities for women. Widening the agenda from a feminist perspective brought gender into focus by placing gender and women as the focus of security calculations and by demonstrating that gender, war and security were intertwined. It was an important development in the rise of a wider perspective on security. Whether one agrees with the wideners or the narrowers, the end of the Cold War indicated that security was an essentially contested concept – 'a concept that generates debates that cannot be resolved by reference to empirical evidence because the concept contains a clear ideological or moral element and defies precise, generally accepted definition' (Fierke 2015, 35). By pointing at the essentially contested nature of security, critical approaches to security argue that 'security' is not necessarily positive or universal, but context and subject dependent and even negative at times.

Because some administer security while others receive security, security produces uneven power relations between people. For example, in the context of the Global War on Terror, a person who looks Arab has been regarded with suspicion as a dangerous 'other' and there has been an increase in surveillance operations in Muslim communities on the presumption that because they fit a certain profile, they may be connected to terrorism. Viewed in this light, surveillance becomes a security apparatus of control and a source of insecurity. It is by questioning the essence of security in cases such as this that securitisation theory developed and widened the scope of security to include other referent objects beyond the state. A referent object, a central idea in securitisation, is the thing that is threatened and needs to be protected.

Securitisation theorists determined five sectors: the economic, the societal, the military, the political and the environmental sector. In each sector, a specific threat is articulated as threatening a referent object. For example, in the societal sector, the referent object is identity, while the referent objects in the environmental sector are the ecosystem and endangered species. It is only in the military sector that the referent object remains the state. By 'sectorialising' security, we understand that existential threats are not objective but instead relate to the different characteristics of each referent object. This technique also highlights the contextual nature of security and threats. Suicide bomb attacks, for example, are a greater source of anxiety for some people today than they are for others. Yet we often hear suicide terrorism framed as a 'global' threat. Securitisation shows that it is incorrect to talk about issues such as terrorism as if they concern everyone around the world equally. By talking about referent objects we can ask: Security for whom? Security from what? And security by whom?

Central to securitisation theory is showing the rhetorical structure of decision-makers when framing an issue and attempting to convince an audience to lift the issue above politics. This is what we call a speech act – 'by saying the words, something is done, like betting, giving a promise, naming a ship'

(Buzan, Wæver and de Wilde 1998, 26). Conceptualising securitisation as a speech act is important as it shows that words do not merely describe reality, but constitute reality, which in turn triggers certain responses. In the process of describing the reality we see, we also interact with that world and perform an action that will greatly contribute to seeing that reality in a different way. For example, referring to an immigration camp in Calais as 'the Jungle' is not simply describing what the camp really is, but portraying it as a lawless and dangerous place. Hence, threats are not just threats by nature, but are constructed as threats through language. In order to convince an audience to take extraordinary measures, the securitising actor must draw attention and often exaggerate the urgency and level of the threat, communicate a point of no return, i.e. 'if we do not tackle this problem, everything else will be irrelevant', and offer a possible way out (lifting the issue above politics) – which is often framed in military terms. In so doing, the securitising actor makes some actions more intelligible than others and enables a regime of truth about the nature of the threat and about the referent object's nature.

An issue becomes securitised when an audience collectively agrees on the nature of the threat and supports taking extraordinary measures. If the audience rejects the securitising actor's speech act, it only represents a securitising move and the securitisation has failed. In this respect, the focus on the audience and on process requires considerably more than simply 'saying security'. This has generated criticism from some scholars, who recommend understanding securitisation as a long process of ongoing social constructions and negotiation between various audiences and speakers. Any security issue can be presented on a spectrum ranging from non-politicised (the issue has not reached public debate) to politicised (the issue has raised public concerns and is on the agenda) to securitised (the issue has been framed as an existential threat). When an issue is securitised, actions are often legitimised under the language of 'urgency' and 'existential threats' and are measures that may be deemed undemocratic in normal situations. Security measures in the War on Terror, such as the Guantanamo Bay detention camp, the use of torture, the increased surveillance of citizens, extraordinary renditions and secretive drone strikes, illustrate the logic of exceptionality. Had the War on Terror not been framed in a context in which a suspension of normal politics was permissible and necessary, these security measures would probably not have existed – nor would they have endured to the present day.

A successful securitisation places 'security' as an exceptional realm, investing securitising actors (nominally states) with the power to decide when the democratic framework should be suspended and with the power to manipulate populations. For Wæver (2015 and 2000), securitisation theory was built to protect politics against the disproportionate power of the state by placing the success and failure of securitisation in the hands of the audience, rather than in the securitising actor. Wæver also voiced his preference for 'desecuritisation' – a return to normal politics. After all, audiences are not complete dupes at the mercy of the securitising actor, and by making the process more transparent, securitisation theory endows the audience with agency and responsibility. In this context, the role of the security analyst moves from objectively analysing the threat to studying the processes by which securitising actors construct a shared understanding of what is collectively recognised as a threat. Securitisation theory is thus not so much involved with answering 'why' an issue has been securitised. It is more important that we be concerned with the conditions that have made the securitisation possible by asking 'how' questions: how has a specific lang-uage enabled the actor to convince the audience of the threat?

Securitisation theory and the Islamic State group in Europe

Following attacks in a range of European cities, the Islamic State group (also known as Daesh, ISIS or ISIL) became a high priority on security agendas from 2015 onwards. The group has been presented as a threat to the security of the state, to the security of individuals in Western Europe and more broadly as a threat to the Western way of life. This means that the securitisation of the Islamic State group affects at least three sectors: the societal, the military and the political. Securitisation theory observes that sometimes in a democracy the government must justify the suspension of normal politics to the public. Hence, if the Islamic State group is securitised in European states, which are regarded as democratic, we should be seeing securitising moves from government officials – a rhetorical justification of why intervention, for instance, is the only way to remove the threat of the Islamic State.

It is important to note that securitising actors are not limited to politicians. Security professionals like the police, intelligence services, customs, immigration services, border guards and the military all play an important role in defining the security landscape. They operate within a field of security characterised by competition over the 'right' knowledge over the threat and other risks associated, as well as competition over the 'right' solution. Although disagreements and confrontation occur between security professionals, Bigo, Bonditti and Olsson (2010, 75–78) argue that they are still guided by a set of common beliefs and practices. Securitising actors take security threats objectively and seek to solve them by undertaking various missions. In addition, there are also functional actors who can influence the dynamic of the field of security but who do not have the power to move an issue above politics. Functional actors are paramount since they help frame storylines about the existentially threatening nature of the issue, often creating divides between 'us' and 'them' – and often implicated in 'othering' processes. Examples of functional actors can be the media, academia, non-governmental agencies and think tanks. It can also include individuals themselves, by telling and sharing stories between friends, families and colleagues. For example, extreme claims made in tabloid newspapers across Europe create a narrative in which the Islamic State group is infiltrating society and working to bring on the demise of the democratic state.

Noticeable examples of securitising moves in the United Kingdom can be found during the House of Commons debate on the motion for British military action in Syria on 2 December 2015. British Prime Minister David Cameron argued that 'we face a fundamental threat to our security' from the threat of the Islamic State group, who 'attack us because of who we are, and not because of what we do' (this was the presentation of the nature of the threat and establishment of a regime of truth). He then said that 'we should not wait any longer' to reduce the threat (this was the point of no return). Finally, he pointed out that it is 'not about whether we want to fight terrorism but about how best we do that' (this was the solution provided).

It is more evident in France, when, after the Paris attacks of 13 November 2015, President Francois Hollande declared that 'France is at war' against an army of jihadists that 'has attacked France because France is a country of liberty' (again, focus on 'what and who we are'). In this framing, the French people are 'a people that is fierce, valiant and courageous' and are victims of such attacks for simply 'being alive'. At the other end of the spectrum is 'them', 'an army of jihadists', of 'coward murderers' who constitute an 'abomination' and 'vile attack' that can only be characterised by 'horror'. A point of no return is invoked when Hollande claims that the Islamic State group is an organisation that 'threatens the whole world' and that this 'is the reason why the destruction of Daesh is a *necessity* for the international community'. Finally, the solution, lifting the issue 'above politics' is offered: 'immediate border controls and a state of emergency have been commanded' (Hollande 2015).

The grammar of the security speech act is discernible. The speech points to the existentially threatening nature of the Islamic State group, a point of no return and a solution which breaks free of the normal democratic processes. In the months after the Paris attacks, Hollande increased French military strikes in Syria and ordered a state of emergency that gave French security forces controversial domestic powers. Hence, we have a case of successful securitisation. It is important to note that when arguing that the Islamic State group is securitised, securitisation theorists do not challenge the existence of the group, or that the group has indeed coordinated attacks in Europe.

Instead, securitisation questions the processes by which this group has come to be viewed as a threat and argues that by naming the group a threat, leaders of European states such as France and the United Kingdom are also implicated in the making of war. In that sense, securitisation highlights how Hollande's securitising speech act does not merely describe a state of affairs 'out there', but constitutes the attacks as an act of war and by doing so, brings war into being. Describing the threat of the Islamic State group is thus not impartial or objective, rather it is in an action in and of itself, and one that should be viewed as a political act.

Using securitisation theory shows that the politics of terrorism and counterterrorism is about threat magnification and that the symbolic violence caused by attacks is out of proportion to the number of deaths it is responsible for. For example, the number of victims in Western Europe was higher in the 1970s and 1980s as a result of groups such as the IRA than the number that can be attributed to Islamic terrorists in recent times. Yet leaders of European countries claim that the world has never faced such 'barbarity', 'horror' and 'atrocity'. This threat magnification demonstrates the exceptionality of the threat, which, in turn, requires urgent and extraordinary responses. Thinking of terrorism in this way is not only detrimental to the deliberative process but also limits our understanding of terrorism more generally.

Conclusion

Securitisation is a useful tool for students in IR as it contests traditional approaches to security that are overly focused on the security of the state, rather than on other referent objects. Adopting a securitisation framework entails challenging hegemonic and taken-for-granted ideas about the universality and objectivity of security and emphasises the ways in which knowledge is not merely 'out there' but is driven by interests. Securitisation theory reminds us that securitisation is not a neutral act but a political one. From that starting point we are able to dig deeper and investigate the various insecurities that are found in international relations.

15

Critical Geography

IRENA LEISBET CERIDWEN CONNON & ARCHIE W. SIMPSON

Critical geography is based upon the notion that humanity has the potential to transform the environment. It challenges the dominant ideologies that characterise international political structures, hence contesting traditional categories and units of analysis in IR such as anarchy, security and the concept of the state. Critical geography is based upon the principle that questions about spatial relations, which refer to how an object located within a particular space relates to another object, are important because political behaviour is embedded in socio-political structures based on ideas about space. Following from this, if scholarship and political behaviour are ingrained in socio-political structures, an objective analysis of international politics becomes impossible. IR theory cannot reflect the global situation from a neutral standpoint. Critical geographers suggest that alternative ways of thinking about space have the potential to change fundamental ideas, theories and approaches that dominate the study of international politics. In turn, they hope that this alternative scholarship will help to transform international politics and reduce human inequality.

The basics of critical geography

Critical geography emerged in the 1970s as a critique of positivism, which is a form of scholarship based upon the idea that the world exists independently of observers. Critical geography is rooted in neo-Marxism and draws upon the ideas of Jürgen Habermas and the Frankfurt school, who expanded upon ideas within classical Marxism by exploring how freedom from inequality could result from peaceful processes rather than revolutionary action. At this time, scholars began examining how dominant political structures and scholarship perpetuated existing political inequalities.

The end of the Cold War in 1991 saw new global economic developments, accompanied by changes in global demographics. In the early 1990s, the increasing importance of non-state actors such as non-governmental organisations and multinational corporations accompanied by increasing ethno-nationalism – whereby nations are defined on the basis of ethnicity rather than civil state membership – fostered new ideas about security and the role of the state.

Critical IR scholarship began focusing on how dominant theories like realism reinforced unequal power relations by favouring the states that dominated international politics. Drawing on the ideas of Ken Booth and Richard Wyn Jones from the Welsh school, they argued that human insecurity was perpetuated by existing political structures (Booth 1991 and 1997). From this, scholars began looking towards critical geography and Lefebvre's (1991) critical theory of space to examine how assumptions about space perpetuated these existing insecurities and inequalities. Two important scholars associated with this are David Harvey and John Agnew, who highlight how traditional conceptions of space decontextualise processes of state formation and cement traditional polarised conceptions of space between East and West, North and South, developing and developed countries in International Relations thinking (Agnew 1994; Harvey 2001 and 2006).

Critical geography offers a means of examining international political behaviour, including the relationship between governments and people, between states at regional and global levels, and between international organisations and states. There are a number of key ideas and concepts within critical geography that offer alternative analyses of international relations. One key idea relates to the notion of territorial space. Philosopher Henry Lefebvre (1991) argued that there are three ways to think about space: in *absolute, relative* and *relational* terms. From an absolute perspective, space is viewed as fixed and measurable. This fixed idea about territory underpins traditional theories of IR. But, if you assume that territory is fixed, it reinforces assumptions about relationships within and between particular territories.

For example, think about how the world is represented on a standard political map. A political map represents the world in terms of individual states separated from each other by territorial borders. An absolute view of global space takes this mode of representation as fixed, meaning it would not consider the possibility of alternative ways of mapping the world. This fixed view also ignores how international politics changed throughout history, altering the shape of the global space as new states and international institutions emerged.

The absolute view of space is not the only option that scholars have for thinking about the international global space. Lefebvre's concept of relative space challenges the absolute view of space. This concept involves thinking about space in a way that views the international space not 'as an "empty container" or fixed space, but one filled with objects and interconnecting relationships' (Meena 2013). Furthermore, a relative view of space views the existence of this space as a result of the relationships between the objects within this space. From this, the ways in which we understand space can be argued to be a product of a particular set of relationships.

For example, if we consider particular spaces in terms of how they relate to other spaces, we can see that when scholars talk about the 'Global South' they are referring to the south in relation to the 'Global North'. Ideas and representations of the 'Global North' and 'Global South', or of 'East' and 'West' are presented as resulting from the polarised relationships that characterised international politics until the end of the Cold War.

A relative view of space can be used to demonstrate the existence of multiple views and alternative ways of conceptualising space from the views of particular states and other international actors. For example, when IR scholars classify all states in the southern hemisphere as representing the Global South, this view fails to acknowledge the differences and complex relationships that exist between states. It leads us to assume that all states in the south are equal in terms of their political and economic power, when this is not the case as powerful states in the Global South like Brazil have far more political and economic power than poorer states like Malawi. It assumes that states in the South also see themselves as existing together on an equal basis with all the other states in the South, which is an oversimplification as it ignores the many economic and political rivalries that exist between different states in this region. It also fails to acknowledge how particular states within the Global South are politically and economically linked to states within the Global North through trade agreements.

A relational view of space suggests that space cannot exist without the perspective of an observer, as objects only exist in terms of their relations with other objects. For example, when we think about a place, we can only think about it in terms of what we know about it. What we know leads us to form opinions which influence the form and shape that the space takes and to the development of arguments that either support or reject pre-existing ideas and political developments. In turn, these opinions influence the political decisions taken by international state actors that shape the global international space. This can be seen, for example, in terms of approving state membership to regional organisations like the European Union. The way that most scholars think about and represent international political space in terms of sovereign states and their territorial borders can therefore be said to be a product of a perspective of space.

Developments in the literature examine how processes of global change and the growth of alternative political organisations, such as transnational environmental movements and indigenous government institutions, have contributed to shaping the contemporary global space (Harvey 2009). One such development looks at how the rise of indigenous government institutions in the Arctic offer alternative views of space that challenge traditional conceptions of international space and look at how Inuit approaches to governance emphasise collective responsibility for the environment beyond state borders (Zellen 2009). Another recent development examines how the expansion of neoliberal capitalism has resulted in rising socio-economic inequality on a global scale, marginalising the poor within and across nation states, with state-based representation in international political institutions contributing to these growing inequalities (Harvey 2009). In addition, as concerns about human security associated with the risks and impacts of global climate change increasingly come to the fore in IR, critical geography can show us how the mainstream ideas about space embedded in international politics and IR theory may serve to perpetuate human inequality and the marginalisation of those most directly at risk from global environmental change. Alternative ideas about space compel scholars to re-assess the global scale of the risks and impacts of climate change and lend support to arguments that call for representational reform in international politics to reduce inequality and to address the increased risks that climate change poses for traditionally marginalised groups, such as for indigenous people.

Critical geography and Inuit views of space

The Inuit are a group of culturally similar indigenous people living in the Arctic regions of Alaska, Canada, Greenland, Denmark and Russia. Their view of territorial space is based upon cultural similarity and use of land for traditional hunting practices rather than nation-state boundaries. The spatial extent of Inuit occupancy of Arctic territory reaches across five states, illustrating their historic sovereignty over a large area. Yet political maps of the world do not represent this area as Inuit territory. Rather, the area that Inuit territory covers is broken down and subsumed within individual state boundaries. When Inuit territories were colonised by European, American and Russian powers, their territories became part of colonial nation-state territories and the Inuit became subject to the colonial state governments. Today, the legacy of colonialism can still be seen in representations of the international political space, as the majority of membership within international political institutions continues to be designated on the basis of sovereign states, resulting in the ongoing political marginalisation of the Inuit.

Without adequate representation at the international political level, Inuit concerns about security and environmental sustainability cannot influence international policy to the same extent that state governments can. Furthermore, the extent to which Inuit interests are represented in the decisions made at the international level is poor. This is especially so when Inuit interests conflict with the interests of governments, such as over pipeline constructions through Inuit territory to transport oil between states. However, by adopting an Inuit perspective of territory that rejects nation-state delineation of the global space, critical geographers can offer alternative definitions of territory and provide more accurate representations.

The Inuit represent only a small segment of the total population of residents within an individual state – for example, only 0.2% of the total Canadian population were registered as Inuit in the 2011 census. But, when thinking about how Arctic sea ice loss (due to climate change) affects the total numbers of Inuit across each of the five nation states by defining territory as consisting of cultural commonality rather than state boundaries, a much spatially larger picture emerges (Huntington 2013). The loss of ice endangers the economic and cultural livelihoods of the Inuit, as it affects hunting activities and puts coastal villages at risk of erosion and flooding.

When viewed from this perspective, the security risk to the wellbeing of people right across such a large area of the globe appears much more prominent than that afforded by most other IR theories. When scholars adopt traditional spatial definitions, they over-simplify the global space and, as we can see in this example, oversimplify the geographic extent of threats to human security. Furthermore, when scholars define space as existing solely of independent states, it limits the examination of the impacts of environmental disaster to simple comparisons between two or more nations, such as between Canada and United States. This undermines differences in the severity of impacts of natural disasters within particular regions of the world. Moreover, this traditional method of analysis also overlooks how the human security threats posed by environmental disasters are not evenly spread within individual state territories. For example, it downplays the fact that the Inuit living in Alaska are at risk of far greater disruption from the effects of melting sea ice than people living in other areas of the United States. It also downplays how coastal communities within Alaska are at a greater risk from the devastation caused by flooding and erosion than communities located within the interior of the state.

Inuit understandings of territorial space can also provide scholars with an alternative tool to make assessments of international political action taken to mitigate the impacts of global environmental change. Critical geographers contend that traditional analyses of patterns of international political activity are prone to focus on actions taken by formal institutions, like the United Nations, that use a nation-state means of political representation – but stress that this places limits on our appreciation of the wider forms of political action that have been taken to mitigate climate change.

For example, the majority of the scholarly analyses of the International Panel on Climate Change (IPCC) in Copenhagen in Denmark in 2009 described how opinions of state representatives regarding action on climate change and emission on greenhouse gases fell into three camps that consisted of: 1) North America and Europe, whose past industrial activities contributed to most of the problems of climate change, 2) industrialising countries such as the BRICS nations, which tended to see no alternative to carbon emissions as a means to fuel economic growth, and 3) poorer countries, which were more likely to disagree to changes on the basis that development and poverty alleviation represented more pressing goals (Meena 2013). However, this mode of analysis is based on divisions of territory defined by tiers of industrial development and ignores differences in influential capacities across and within nations grouped within each tier – for example, between Brazil and China, or between large segments of the South African population.

Over-simplistic ways of thinking about the international political space lead to a lack of consideration for alternative forms of political action, particularly action that takes place outside formal international political institutions including that taken by indigenous organisations, whose spheres of representation and governance transcend nation state boundaries. For example, the Inuit are members of the Arctic Council, which is an international governmental organisation that addresses issues faced by Arctic governments and indigenous people. The Inuit take prominent decision-making roles in the Council rather than having their participation restricted to mere observer status – as at the United Nations climate summits. The decisions the Inuit take are based upon their sense of commonality that transcends state boundaries. Because of their influence in the Arctic Council they have been able to achieve success in fostering a culture of collective governance on environmental management by seeking discussion and resolution of a matter of common concern to all Inuit.

However, despite the success of Inuit representation in the Arctic Council, the vast majority of indigenous governmental bodies continue to fall outside the formal political representational structure in larger international climate change negotiations. The Inuit Circumpolar Council (ICC) is a United Nations-recognised non-governmental organisation that defines its constituency as Inuit populations in Greenland, Alaska, Canada and Russia. However, their participation is restricted at UN summits on climate change to that of 'observer' status as it is not a sovereign state – thereby constraining its voice. It is on this basis that the state system of representation within the United Nations climate summits can be argued to further marginalise indigenous groups like the Inuit. As representation is afforded on the basis of state territory rather than Inuit conceptions of territory it reinforces the decision-making power of the former colonial governments, enabling them to exercise greater control over international affairs, which hinders Inuit self-determination efforts.

The power of the Inuit to shape international political decision-making risks becoming further marginalised if IR scholarship does not critically question nation-state ideas about territory and representation. By bringing alternative conceptualisations of territory to the foreground, critical geography opens up a space for recognising and exploring alternative modes of representation that reduce inequality between indigenous people and state governments. If the Inuit are at greater direct risk from the impacts of global climate change, representational reform would enable them to have a greater voice in managing these risks.

Conclusion

By drawing attention to alternative ways that space can be imagined, critical geographers have sought to transform international politics and the global space. Critical geography highlights how issues of economics and climate change impact upon people and shows that the spatial effects of these processes differ to how they are dealt with by states, international organisations and within academia. The unique vantage point of critical geography provides useful ways to rethink what we know about International Relations in both theoretical and empirical terms. It challenges assumptions about space and territory, offers new conceptual and analytical tools and encourages students to question mainstream thinking.

16

Asian Perspectives

PICHAMON YEOPHANTONG

With the emergence of the so-called 'Asian Century', which sees rising powers like China and India assume a more prominent role in shaping world affairs, Asia has become an important region of study. These global trends have been matched by new directions in scholarship, whereupon Asia has become a conceptual anchor for the development of non-Western approaches to the study of world politics. It is, therefore, within the Asian IR context that some of the most exciting theoretical challenges to, and innovations in, IR scholarship are being mounted and produced. Given the vast socio-cultural and political diversity found across the continent, Asian IR is made up of an array of different perspectives. Some originate in countries in the Global South while others, such as Japanese perspectives, do not. Asian IR therefore feeds into Global South IR perspectives, but remains distinct from them, just as it speaks to mainstream IR theories but is founded on unique political traditions and practices.

The basics of Asian perspectives

IR theory is primarily based on assumptions derived from Western modes of thinking and viewing the world. This, in turn, renders it 'too narrow in its sources and too dominant in its influence' (Acharya and Buzan 2010, 2). The result of this is that non-Western perspectives and theoretical insights have been systematically neglected or ignored altogether by the discipline. For many scholars, this silence of non-Western IR voices constitutes a profound cause of concern, and one that casts a doubtful light on the utility of mainstream theories as a lens to make sense of a complex and culturally diverse world. Consider the English school of IR. The key concepts under-pinning the English school and its conception of 'international society' – for example, the principles of national sovereignty and sovereign equality – are founded upon the historical European experience. China, for one, only learnt these concepts through its encounter with the colonial-era European powers, as was also the case for other Asian countries. The Chinese empire had, until then, conducted its dealings with other nations on the basis of a Sinocentric worldview, where it acted as the political and cultural centre of the world, with the Chinese emperor seen to rule over *Tianxia* or 'All-under-Heaven' (basically, the rest of the world). Sovereign equality never existed as a concept to the Chinese mind until the nineteenth century. Given the distinctive histories, cultures and interstate dynamics seen in Asia, we clearly cannot take for granted the universality of the assumptions and concepts prevalent in IR scholarship.

Asian perspectives on interstate politics exist – and have existed – for millennia. Ancient Indian and Chinese political theorists like Kautilya (circa 300 BCE) and Confucius (551–479 BCE) have provided some salient observations on foreign policy. It would only be in the mid-1990s, when efforts began to make IR scholarship more representative, that the contributions of these thinkers started to be taken seriously by the discipline. In the years since, we are seeing language barriers being broken down along with growing theoretical innovation challenging old thinking in IR. Discussions have converged on the feasibility of constructing various schools and theories of Chinese, Japanese, Korean and Southeast Asian IR – among other possibilities. As such, though still mired in debate and a degree of uncertainty, the ultimate outcome of these discussions will prove central to the future of IR as a global discipline.

At present, there is no single, unifying, pan-Asian school or theory of International Relations. Various reasons can be given for why this is the case. For example, the 'hidden' nature of non-Western IR theories, referring to the difficulty of recognising non-Western perspectives even when we see them (Acharya and Buzan 2010, 18) – or the failure to challenge the theoretical 'imports' and acknowledge the value of non-Western theory-building (Puchala 1997, 132; Chun 2010, 83). There is, of course, nothing inherently 'Western' about IR theorising. But whether we can rightly speak about an Asian IR theory depends in large part on how we define 'theory' and understand 'Asian'.

In this light, Asian IR should not be viewed as a self-contained, monolithic discourse, nor as an intellectual enterprise aimed purely at the production of grand theories. Although having garnered plenty of attention in non-Western IR scholarship, the Chinese and Japanese schools of IR represent but two strands of Asian thought among several others. Rather than 'theory' in the sense of advancing testable observations about how the international system operates, it may be better to describe the bulk of Asian IR approaches as perspectives for making sense of the world. This, in turn, raises the important question of whether a unified Asian IR theory is in fact desirable. Siddharth Mallavarapu (2014), for one, is less interested in putting forward monolithic theories, being more 'curious about how the world is viewed from this particular location'. Navnita Chadha Behera (2010, 92) likewise rejects the notion of creating an Indian school of IR out of concern that such an undertaking would result in a 'self-other binary' that simply pits Indian IR (self) against Western IR (other). This speaks to a broader concern that the construction of unified schools of thought risks creating grossly simplified and polarising categories that end up supplanting one dominant body of knowledge with another. Similar sentiments also pervade debates on the Chinese school, with some scholars remaining sceptical about the feasibility of a single school representing the diversity of Chinese perspectives.

Conceptual pluralism better serves the original intention of non-Western IR theorists – that is, to bring diversity back into the study of world politics. Following from this, it is also important that we don't overstate the differences between Western and Asian IR approaches. Indeed, a common attribute of Asian and Western approaches lies with their normative qualities – that is, their interest in how the world *ought* to be. Kautilya, for example, noted the necessity of waging a just war (for example, for a king not to take the land of an ally), whereas Confucian scholars were concerned with how to sustain 'harmony' (peace and stability) in the world through able statecraft.

Much like Western IR theories, Asian perspectives have deep roots in political thought. In many cases, it is a matter of transposing theories of statecraft, society and human nature to the global realm. Just as Enlightenment-era philosophers like Thomas Hobbes and John Locke were central to the development of IR theory, ancient and modern philosophers from Confucius and Sun Tzu (544–496 BCE) to Shiratori Kurakichi (1865–1942) and Nishida Kitarō (1870–1945) are important sources of inspiration for Asian scholars.

According to Benoy Kumar Sarkar (1919), early Hindu political theorists already had an indigenous conception of sovereignty that recognised the importance of 'self-rule' and national independence to the exercise of state authority. The Indian statesman and philosopher Kautilya, who is often lauded as one of the world's earliest realists, is a critical figure in this regard. In setting out the principles of conduct central to the task of empire-building, his mandala (spheres of influence) theory advanced ideas as to how a king should manage alliances and relations of enmity with surrounding countries. It acknowledged, for instance, the utility of non-intervention as a means for building confidence between kings and avoiding unnecessary foreign entanglements, having also proposed an early conceptualisation of 'strength' as a tool for attaining 'happiness' (Vivekanandan 2014, 80).

Similarly, elements of Confucian thinking on power, order and statecraft can be distilled from how China conducts its foreign policy today. The importance of maintaining harmony to safeguarding the global order is a Confucian concept that remains a popular refrain in China. Similarly, the notion that to wield power a state must shoulder commensurate domestic and international responsibilities is one that defines China's contemporary identity as a responsible stakeholder. It has also served as the basis for the corresponding 'responsibility thesis', which advances the notion that China has certain unavoidable duties and obligations as a rising power, particularly with respect to managing and securing global order and stability (Yeophantong 2013).

In seeking to identify its own unique contributions to the field, Japanese IR has also drawn extensively upon the works of celebrated philosophers, including Nishida Kitarō, who was the pioneer of the Kyoto School. Often labelled as a 'proto-constructivist' due to the prominence he gave to cultural factors and identity construction, Nishida advanced a philosophy of identity for addressing a fundamental Japanese conundrum of whether Japan belongs to the East or the West. Here, he adopted a dialectic approach, arguing that Japanese identity exists within a 'coexistence of opposites, Eastern and Western', which consequently allows it to cultivate a universal appeal (Inoguchi 2007, 379). In other words, Japan is accorded a special role in the world, as it is positioned to encourage both Eastern and global awareness. This argument fits with Nishida's broader vision of a multicultural world, where a 'true world culture' was to be achieved through the recognition of cultural difference and the union of these differences (Krummel 2015, 218).

Despite criticism against their hegemonic position in the discipline, it warrants note how mainstream IR theories have helped to provide fertile ground for new ideas and approaches to germinate among Asian IR scholars. South Korean IR scholars, for example, have been heavily influenced by mainstream IR – specifically, its theories that are focused on addressing real-world issues. The rationale behind efforts to build a Chinese IR School also stems from the desire to better represent Chinese ideas and interests within an American-dominated discipline. It is possible, however, to divide Chinese IR scholars working in the pre-1949 period and during the 1980s-90s into two camps (Lu 2014): those who sought to learn from and emulate Western theories and those who used Western IR as the basis for critique and the development of alternative perspectives.

It is interesting to recall how Samuel Huntington's 1993 'Clash of Civilizations' article, which argued that culturally driven conflicts will invariably define the post-Cold War world, had sparked heated discussion within China during the mid-1990s due to its controversial speculation of a coming conflict between the West and 'Confucian-Islamic' states. Not only did this lead to a deepening of Chinese dissatisfaction with Western theories and their misrepresentations of Eastern cultures, it also gave Chinese scholars renewed impetus to establish a Chinese school of IR.

You are probably wondering, if there is no Asian IR theory, then can Asian perspectives really provide a (more) compelling account of interstate dynamics than mainstream IR theories?

Certainly, we can view the lack of a unifying set of core theoretical assumptions as a sizeable limitation of current Asian IR approaches. While we can easily identify the major tenets of realism or constructivism, Asian perspectives tend to exhibit a greater degree of conceptual fluidity and context-specificity. In practical terms, however, there are instances where Asian IR has made noteworthy contributions to 'middle-range theorising' (the formulation of fact-driven theories to explain a specific real-world phenomenon) and 'soft IR theory', which refers to the policy-driven theories informed by the 'thinking and foreign policy approaches of Asian leaders' (Acharya and Buzan 2010, 11). These are normally relied upon to generate policy prescriptions, as well as insights into the factors that motivate the foreign-policy behaviour of Asian states.

An influential middle-range theory is Akamatsu Kaname's 'flying geese model' of regional development. Not only has the theory been used to justify Japan's economic leadership within Asia (Korhonen 1994), but it also serves as the rationale behind the country's economic assistance to developing countries. Kaname posited the theory in the 1930s to explain how a developing country can catch up with industrialised countries through their interactions. With Japan's rapid industrialisation from the late nineteenth century onwards and the remarkable economic development of East Asian countries in the post-Second World War period, Japan came to be depicted within this theory as the 'lead goose' in a V-shaped formation comprised of emerging Asian economies. Here, Japan helped to stimulate regional industrialisation and economic growth by passing down its older technology and know-how (through economic assistance programmes, for instance) to other developing countries.

An example of a soft theoretical contribution is the concept of 'non-alignment' (not taking sides). Developed by India's Jawaharlal Nehru against the backdrop of divisive Cold War politics, non-alignment became an influential policy framework adopted by Asian and African countries that had sought to occupy the middle ground between the rival powers during the 1950s and 1960s.

Asian perspectives on developing a Chinese school of IR

In China, the construction of a Chinese school of IR theory has become a national preoccupation that resonates strongly with China's global aspirations. At a time when the Chinese government is emphasising the country's rich cultural – namely, Confucian – heritage in official rhetoric, Chinese IR scholars are increasingly turning to ancient Chinese political thought for insights that transcend both time and geography.

Although having been in development since the late 1920s, early attempts to build a Chinese school can be traced back to the late 1950s, when the focus of academic debates began to earnestly shift from learning from the West to rejecting Western IR and developing a distinct Chinese IR approach. This shift crystallised with the rift in Sino-Soviet relations during the 1960s, 1970s and 1980s, whereupon the Soviet Union's approach to IR was officially denounced within China. The late 1980s saw a clearer division emerge between Chinese scholars who favoured Western IR approaches and those who pushed for IR theory with Chinese characteristics. Maoist scholars like Liang Shoude argued for the rejection of Western theories and the development of a Chinese model instead. Subsequent debates in the early 2000s largely centred on the hegemonic status of Western IR. Here, the notion of establishing a Chinese school replaced the more ideologically driven objective of theorising with Chinese characteristics.

The Chinese school project thus came to be defined not only in opposition to a 'prejudiced' IR discipline, but also in light of the challenges faced by China as a rising power within an American-dominated, globalising world (Wang and Han 2016, 54). It is in this way that Chinese IR perspectives draw upon Western IR theories, while being equally coloured by Maoist-socialist ideas, ancient Chinese political thought and China's own experiences in navigating the international terrain.

According to Qin Yaqing (2016), a theory of 'relationality' postulates that states as social actors base their actions on the nature of the relations they have with others. The logic of relationality thus dictates that 'an actor tends to make decisions according to the degrees of intimacy and/or importance of her relationships to specific others' (Qin 2016, 37). This logic is founded upon ancient Chinese philosophy that emphasises the importance of respecting, and behaving in line with, the hierarchy of relationships (e.g. between the emperor and heaven, king and subject, father and son) to social and even cosmological stability. But of particular significance here is the relationship between the two opposite forces, *yin* and *yang,* which is seen to govern all other relationships. The existence of *yin* is seen as dependent on *yang*, which effectively makes them two complementary halves of a whole. This notion of inclusivity – that 'each of a pair is inclusive of the other' (Qin 2016, 40) – is central to the concept of *Zhongyong* ('the Middle Course'), which suggests how opposites give rise to positive interactions, rendering harmony, not conflict, as the state of nature. The theory of relationality is one that seeks to explain how contradictions can coexist and also how their coexistence is necessary to functioning relationships. Considering how world politics operates on the basis of ambivalent relationships, where a state can be perceived as an ally one moment and a threat the next, relationality becomes a useful theory.

Take, for example, the relationship between China and the Philippines. Political ties between these two countries, while longstanding, have been frayed due to their competing territorial claims over a chain of islands and atolls in the South China Sea, which are believed to hold valuable gas deposits and strategic importance. As both countries have become ever bolder in their attempts to assert ownership over the islands, tensions have flared. In 2016, the Philippines won an arbitration case that concluded that China has no legal basis to claim historic rights to the South China Sea. The Chinese government strongly rejected the Permanent Court of Arbitration's ruling. Speculations soon emerged of a coming military conflict between the two countries. Yet, no military conflict occurred. Despite animosity on both sides over this issue, economic relations between China and the Philippines continue to grow.

From the perspective of relationality, both political tension and economic cooperation constitute the Sino-Philippine relationship. Applying the Zhongyong concept, one can assume that conflict is *not* unavoidable within this relationship. If anything, military conflict would constitute an aberration to the status quo – something that is costly to both sides. Such a prospect could thus serve to compel China and the Philippines to seek out new avenues for conflict resolution and cooperation as a means to restore balance between the oppositional forces within the relationship. Shortly after the arbitration ruling, Philippine president Rodrigo Duterte articulated his desire to negotiate directly with China on the South China Sea issue, even proposing joint resource development in the contested waters and urging the Chinese government to assist the Philippines with infrastructure development. A Chinese white paper (2017) published after the ruling, while reaffirming China's claims in the South China Sea, reiterated Beijing's commitment to settling the dispute via negotiation and consultation.

Via a relationality perspective, we can expect that harmonious contradictions will continue to characterise the Sino-Philippine relationship, as cooperation between the two countries persists despite tensions. This is an important demonstration of the value of the Chinese school as it runs contrary to what mainstream IR theorists, who ground their analyses of interstate interactions in a conflictual state of international anarchy, would lead us to expect.

Conclusion

As International Relations is an increasingly popular subject, particularly in Asia where IR courses have become a staple at many universities, there is a need for it to become a truly global discipline that appreciates political and cultural difference but also reflects a shared history and humanity. In light of the uncertainties and anxieties accompanying the rise of non-Western powers like China and India, IR scholarship must act not only as a lens for analysing real-world phenomena but also as a useful and practical guide for how we should act within a changing global environment. That said, 'Asia' is as much a social construct as 'the West' and one that could potentially become as monolithic and hegemonic. As such, we need to be wary of creating simplistic categories that give rise to an unhelpful 'self–other' binary. For the sake of initiating meaningful dialogue, it is vital that scholars continue to work towards an inclusive outlook that reconciles East and West, capturing both the diversity and unity of insights to be gained from mainstream as well as Asian IR perspectives.

17

Global South Perspectives

LINA BENABDALLAH, CARLOS MURILLO-ZAMORA
& VICTOR ADETULA

The Global South is generally understood to refer to less economically developed countries. It is a broad term that comprises a variety of states with diverse levels of economic, cultural, and political influence in the international order. Although International Relations is an interdisciplinary field of study, it has historically been studied from a very Eurocentric perspective that does not always help us to understand developments occurring in the Global South. Understanding Global South perspectives starts with a discussion of the Western-centric focus of mainstream IR theories. It also recognises the challenges facing scholars from the Global South that might help to explain why Global South perspectives are largely absent from mainstream debates. The ultimate goal is to broaden the field of view within IR theory to incorporate a more just and representative understanding of international relations.

The basics of Global South perspectives

The main weakness of mainstream Western IR theories is that they are not universally experienced as mainstream. The concepts they are based on do not unequivocally reflect or match the reality in many Global South states. Furthermore, certain questions that are central to Global South perspectives are absent or under-theorised in mainstream scholarship. Tickner (2016, 1) for example points out that issues of race and empire have been missing from mainstream theories despite the existence of solid scholarship in postcolonial and poststructuralist studies. Curiously, she adds, colonial dominations profoundly shaped the state of the current global order, yet they are not even remotely central to mainstream IR. Today, there is a growing body of scholarship that pays attention to the context of international relations theories in Africa, Asia and Latin America and to the diverse interpretations within these vast regions. Much of this scholarship has been produced under the umbrella term of 'global IR'.

Mainstream IR also gets it wrong in its reading of history. When major global events are told from a Western perspective, the voices of the colonised and oppressed often go missing, which leads to a different basis for theorising. For example, realist scholarship refers to the Cold War as a period of relative stability given that no major war was fought between the two superpowers, the United States and the Soviet Union. However, if one looks at the same period through a Global South lens, one can see a world full of proxy wars and human suffering where both superpowers intervened in conflicts to support their interests or damage those of the other. A simple example like this highlights two issues for mainstream scholarship. On the one hand, it is important to incorporate non-Western actors and non-Western thinking in order to explore the ways in which different actors challenge, support, and shape global and regional orders. On the other hand, it is also important to question the relevance of mainstream theories to the context of postcolonial states and theorise the role of emerging economies and other Global South states in shaping international institutions and global governance. So, the prevailing questions are whether traditional IR theories are able to adapt to Global South perspectives, and if not whether new theories and approaches are needed in their place. In answering this question, scholars have taken a wide range of different positions.

While many scholars are united around a call for justice and equality in the way that IR narratives represent the world, it cannot be said that there is one grand strategy for theorising Global South perspectives. This dilemma is perhaps best illustrated by the question, 'who are the Global South scholars?' In many cases it would be inaccurate to refer to a single perspective that could be seen to represent a region or even country, let alone the majority of the world's population. While they may share similar experiences of exploit-ation under colonisation, can such a term as 'African' be used to describe the diverse experiences of states ranging from Malawi to Morocco? Scholars do not even agree on a single definition of which states the 'Latin American' region comprises let alone what a Latin American perspective on international relations might mean. Similarly, it has proved difficult to define a coherent theoretical body that would constitute a 'Chinese school' of Intern-ational Relations, given the array of different philosophers and interpretations of their work that might encompass. Issues like these make it difficult for Global South scholars to rally around a single theoretical perspective.

While one unifying goal might be to challenge the domination of the Global North, then a further risk of fragmentation lies in the power asymmetries between Global South states themselves. Inequalities are not exclusive to North/South relations but also permeate relations between states of the South. The emergence of strong economies and regional powers within the Global South such as China, Brazil and India has raised new issues of marginalisation and dominance among states *already* marginalised by the North.

A further challenge comes in the historical dominance of Western means of knowledge production and publication. If there is little talk of an African theoretical perspective in IR, for example, this is perhaps more indicative of the impact of Western imperialism on indigenous systems of knowledge production in Africa than of a lack of African theorists. Indeed, the continent of Africa is home to age-old experiences and practices in diplomacy and intergovernmental relations that long predate the arrival of the Europeans in the colonial era. Yet, during colonisation many states were subject to the domination of Western forms of knowledge that consciously or inadvertently imposed certain values on the colonies.

Even since independence, scholarly outputs have tended to reflect Western concerns and experiences, even sometimes when being written from within the Global South. An example of this can be seen in the development of IR scholarship in Latin America. Ever since the Monroe Doctrine of 1823, which stated the United States' intent to keep European powers out of the Americas, the United States has adopted a policy towards its nearest neighbours that sees Latin America as its strategic backyard, and has regularly resulted in interventionist actions. In spite of notable efforts, much teaching and research about Latin America has been written in or for the United States. This is exacerbated by the fact that to secure careers, scholars need to publish in prestigious English-language publications, which are often based in the United States.

By shining a spotlight on the forgotten past of the pre-colonial era, Global South scholars can demonstrate the injustices of the present. For example, when told from a Western perspective, accounts of African histories begin with the arrival of the Europeans. Yet the accounts of early European explorers themselves towards the end of the fourteenth century testify to the political structures, institutions and organisations that were already in place in many areas. Africa was the site of empires, kingdoms and other social institutions that made it possible for trade, commerce and religion to thrive. The records of early Arab travellers and traders across the Sahara Desert make reference to the diplomatic activities of some early kingdoms and empires in West Africa, notably the Ghana empire, the Mali empire, the Songhai empire and Islamic missionaries who used the trans-Sahara trade routes. In the course of their travels, colonial missionaries form Europe reported that the networks of trade and commerce across the Sahara Desert had successfully bridged North Africa with Europe. Clearly, trade, commerce, diplomatic activities as well as learning and knowledge production were at various levels of development in Africa before the coming of the Europeans. Yet, narratives that start with colonisation see African states as only being independent and 'sovereign' since decolonisation in the mid-twentieth century. They are therefore seen to be 'new states', which only very recently became part of the contemporary international system. This 'newness' is used to defend international institutions that exclude African states from power structures and decision-making systems – such as key bodies of the United Nations like the Security Council – on the grounds that the rules for managing inter-state relations were established long before the establishment of most African states. However, if attention is paid to the histories the West 'forgot', then this becomes more difficult to justify. As a result, many African countries are at the forefront of the campaign for the restructuring of the United Nations and the work of Global South scholars is helping to build their case.

Global South perspectives on international development

Many of the policies that shape international politics today are based on assumptions that originate in Western modes of thinking. Take, for example, 'development' – a word that has the power to dictate national and international policies and attract or divert vast sums of money. This can be seen through the United Nations' Millennium Development Goals and their successors, the Sustainable Development Goals. These involve targets that every country in the world agreed to strive towards and to fund. They are based on an understanding of development that sees many countries in the Global South as not having yet achieved the economic progress of the North.

Perhaps one of the greatest contributions of Latin American scholars to IR theory is dependency theory, which challenges dominant understandings of development as an organising principle in international politics. Dependency theory asserts that underdevelopment and poverty are the result of political, economic and cultural influences exerted on such countries from the outside. It presents the relationship between the Global South and the Global North as exploitative and unfair by underlining the ways in which states in the South have been incorporated into the world economic system through capitalist development, which has exploited human and material resources and disrupted indigenous modes of production. Dependency theory analyses the way in which the underdevelopment of many states in the South might be a direct result of the policies, interventions and unfair trading practices of states from the North. From this perspective, the current (unfair) economic relations between the Global North and South will not help the South to develop at all. Rather, they will keep the South poorer than the North. Rather than the need for states in the Global South to 'develop', dependency theory stresses that nothing short of a restructuring of the entire international economic system will deliver economic justice for the world's poor.

Building on the likes of dependency theory, scholars have demonstrated that the economic exploitation of many colonised nations did not stop with decolonisation. In fact, in the final years of colonialism – at the time when independence movements were becoming too strong to suppress – the departing colonial powers instigated a number of policies and programmes that paved the way for a new type of domination of Global South economies. The legacy of such policies was an emphasis on the production of cash crops for export, dependence on foreign financial interventions and the entrench-ment of private capital (both domestic and foreign) as the engine of growth and development. North–South trade agreements and the policies of international organisations such as the World Trade Organization have further served to protect the interests of established powers despite repeated calls from the South for a fairer deal in global trade relations. They have served to privilege 'developed' states in trade relationships and to disadvantage the former 'developing' colonies. Viewed from the North, such policies are an instrument for helping the South. However, viewed from the South, they are tantamount to a new type of colonial domination – often referred to as 'neo-colonialism' – in that they represent a continuation of unequal and exploitative North–South relationships.

Mainstream IR theories emerging from Western societies largely seek rational explanations for states' interactions. However, some scholars have started to explore the motivations behind interactions between states in the Global South from a relational perspective. An example of this emphasis on relationality can be seen in China's interactions with various African states. In 2015 China became the African continent's largest trading partner. Chinese investments across Africa include natural resource extractions, infrastructure construction, real estate and information technology. African and Chinese economies are mutually interdependent in that China imports a lot of energy sources from the continent and African states in return import consumer goods, commodities, and technology from China. Most African states, however, import far more than they export to China and suffer from un-balanced trade relations. China's development model (the Beijing Consensus) differs from the neoliberal model of development advocated by the Inter-national Monetary Fund and other Western-led organisations (the Washington Consensus). The Washington Consensus' emphasis on liberal-isation and minimising the role of the state in the market has been denounced by many African leaders as neocolonial and exploitative. By contrast, the Beijing Consensus, with its emphasis on the principle of non-interference, has presented an attractive alternative to some African countries.

Furthermore, while China certainly benefits economically from its developmental role in African states, enhancing cultural dialogue and cultivating networks through people-to-people exchanges also seem to be important motivating factors behind its interventions. As well as funding Confucius Institutes across the continent of Africa showcasing Chinese language and culture, the Chinese government has sponsored 200,000 opportunities for training professionals, academics, journalists and public servants from all corners of Africa. It is part of constructing a shared identity based on future aspirations and trajectories that will lift citizens out of poverty. Whether or not China's approach in Africa is in fact a genuinely new type of development policy is subject to heated debate among scholars. But the point here is that China is keen to be seen to adopt a more relational approach, as opposed to the rational one of the North. Indeed, this concept is not exclusively Chinese – it also extends to other societies within the Global South and offers an alternative way of theorising South–South relations to the perspectives that have emerged from the North.

Conclusion

In recent years a lot has been done to highlight the important contributions that actors from the Global South make, and have always made, to international relations. Indeed, IR as a discipline has come a long way in incorporating aspects, actors and concepts that represent the world more widely. Yet, as the dynamics of the international system continue to change with the emergence of new economic powers such as India, China, Brazil, Turkey as well as other rising economies, IR will need to do more to pay attention to the perspectives of those in the South. Global South perspectives not only challenge the dominant theoretical perspectives that have served to create and perpetuate unjust relations between the Global North and South, they also open up the possibility of different, fairer relations that represent the interests of all concerned and challenge international institutions to have more representative power structures and decision-making processes.

18

Indigenous Perspectives

JEFF CORNTASSEL & MARC WOONS

Being Indigenous is about honouring and renewing complex relationships between humans and also with the natural world. The United Nations offers a multifaceted working definition of what it means to be a member of one of the thousands of Indigenous nations living around the world. It includes factors like self-identification, historical continuity and a place-based existence that links to a particular territory. The definition also speaks to distinct governance systems, languages, historical experiences, cultures and ways of knowing. Importantly, it additionally describes communities that seek to maintain their territories and assert themselves as distinct peoples – despite their existence within a state (usually against their wishes). States, on the other hand are constructed around different principles of territorial sovereignty and legally recognised governmental systems and have historically sought to control, coerce, and even eliminate Indigenous peoples from the landscape. The existing, dominant framework of inter-state relations roots itself in state sovereignty. From an Indigenous perspective this has been established through violence, broken treaties and other unjust assertions of power over Indigenous peoples and their lands. This undermines, downplays, excludes and ultimately provokes Indigenous worldviews and counter-arguments that seek to push the state-centric model beyond its narrow confines. By exploring Indigenous perspectives and complex relationships we can more clearly see the problems that come from the many assumptions at the heart of International Relations and its family of theories.

The basics of Indigenous perspectives

The current dominant global political and legal order, invented in Europe, is state-centric and has since spread everywhere to create the discrete borders that mark the geopolitical world map most use today. Putting an end to decades of brutal violence and endemic conflict throughout Europe, the 1648 Peace of Westphalia cemented the totalising and enduring notion of state sovereignty. Europe's response to anarchy, conflict and disorder among nations (or peoples) was thus the creation of a system of inter-state relations bolstered by states mutually recognising one another's sovereign authority. Indigenous understandings of international relations differ from inter-state approaches, particularly when it comes to the ways that Indigenous peoples renew and act on their sacred commitments and interdependencies with the natural world. Assertions of Indigenous resurgence, which entails reclaiming and regenerating relationships with lands, cultures and communities, promote positive, alternative visions of the international that challenge the dominant inter-state model.

The concept of state sovereignty fuelled modern state-building strategies and, almost without exception, led to the destruction of Indigenous nations. Each state tries to build a vision of a common people sharing a culture, values, history, language, currency (and so on) through education, military conquest and other state-driven initiatives. This is often called a national identity, and is associated with ideas like patriotism and nationalism. Indigenous encounters with European empires saw them time and again face a stark choice (if the choice was even put to them at all): assimilate to the new settler colonial order being imposed over them and their lands or face dislocation – even genocide. As George Manuel and Michael Posluns (1974, 60) point out,

> the colonial system is always a way of gaining control over another people for the sake of what the colonial power has determined to be 'the common good.' People can only become convinced of the common good when their own capacity to imagine ways in which they can govern themselves has been destroyed.

Speaking to Indigenous battles over state-building efforts that alienate Indigenous peoples from their lands and resources, Manuela Picq (2015) suggests that Indigenous perspectives offer three specific challenges to the state-centric perspective. First, they challenge the state's ultimate authority by asserting their authority over their nations, lands/waters, and the natural world. Second, they expose the colonial foundations of the state-centric system by highlighting Indigenous views that both challenge and sit outside the dominant system. In other words, states as we know them owe their existence to processes of colonisation and settlement rooted in cultural imperialism, violence, destruction, genocide and ultimately the eradication of Indigenous identities and relationships to the land if not the eradication of the peoples themselves. Third, Indigenous peoples' worldviews and practices challenge us to imagine what it might be like to share power within and think beyond state borders and the prevailing global state system.

The principle of self-determination has provided stateless Indigenous nations with ways to attempt to (re)assert and (re)claim their authority. Self-determination provides an avenue for Indigenous peoples to create political entities that can be recognised by the international community. The process is based on the idea that people should be free to form their own governments and control their own affairs – something central to the ethics and legality underpinning the United Nations. Indigenous claims of this nature have gained significant traction over the past century, especially post-1945 when decolonisation became a key international process. The sources of self-determining authority are admittedly a source of contention. For Indigenous nations it emanates from complex relationships with their homelands, waters, sacred living histories, animal nations, plant nations, ceremonies, languages and the natural world. The sources of self-determining authority for states are much different, originating from colonial policies. For instance, the Doctrine of Discovery, dating back to the fifteenth century, espouses that land occupied by non-Christians could be legally 'discovered' and claimed as territory owned by the Crown. Other invented political and legal constructs have also become embedded within state legal histories and practices, shaping international practices that deny alternative Indigenous conceptions of relations between nations.

One example of the tension between state sovereignty and Indigenous self-determination can be seen in the story of Cayuga chief Deskaheh's European visit, first to the United Kingdom in 1921 and then to the League of Nations in 1923. In his capacity as the Speaker of the Six Nations of the Haudeno-saunee, he felt compelled to make the long trans-Atlantic journey as conflicts between the Haudenosaunee and Canadian peoples had reached an impasse. He felt it unjust that his people were being imprisoned for protesting the Canadian state's imposition of its self-declared sovereignty over their lands, claiming it to be tantamount to an invasion and stating that 'we are determined to live the free people that we were born' (League of Nations 1923, 3). The lands were, and still are, subject to treaties expressing an alternative vision of shared authority over shared lands and mutual respect between peoples as equal nations cooperatively governing the same territory – an idea that is largely antithetical to the Westphalian vision of exclusive territorial authority by one people. However, Chief Deskaheh's appeals fell on deaf ears in both London and Geneva as the states concerned refused to interfere in the domestic affairs of one of their peers, namely Canada (Corntassel 2008). He eventually left Europe empty-handed, dying soon after in 1925 in New York state, exiled from his homeland that had by then been all but overrun by the Canadian settler state.

Some progress has been made since Chief Deskaheh's time and now appears in prominent places. The UN Declaration on the Rights of Indigenous

Peoples (UNDRIP) urges states to recognise that 'Indigenous peoples have the right to self-determination. By virtue of that right they freely determine their political status and freely pursue their economic, social and cultural development' (United Nations General Assembly 2007: 3). There is also momentum within the United Nations to support what many consider the heart of self-determination – namely, an Indigenous veto over all matters affecting them, their communities and their territories. On the surface, the Declaration seems to secure for Indigenous nations powers previously extended only to states. As White Face (2013) points out, conspiring states refused to adopt it until it included limiting language that eventually made its way into Article 46, which states that 'nothing in this declaration may be interpreted … or construed as authorizing or encouraging any action which would dismember or impair, totally or in part, the territorial integrity or political unity of sovereign and independent states' (United Nations General Assembly 2007: 14). Article 46 can be seen as perpetuating the above-mentioned Doctrine of Discovery or at least its impacts despite its formal repudiation in 2012. Unfortunately, the legal fictions of the Doctrine of Discovery via Article 46 of the UNDRIP as well as other inter-state legal instruments continue to impact Indigenous nations in profound and destructive ways that undermine their self-determining authority (Miller et al. 2010; Special Rapporteur 2010).

Indigenous self-determination should not be confused with the self-determination efforts of non-state nations like Québec, Catalonia, Palestine or Kurdistan. Hoping to achieve the successes of East Timor or South Sudan, these national movements desire a state of their own so that they can be included as fully-fledged members within the inter-state system as it currently exists. Indigenous self-determination movements, on the other hand, mount a more robust and fundamental challenge to the system itself. Even if most Indigenous nations do not seek its wholesale elimination, they strive for ways of being included on their own terms that tend to reject the Westphalian idea of state sovereignty. Given that there are approximately 5,000 Indigenous nations throughout the world, there are many ways of asserting self-determining authority. Many Indigenous alternatives even reject the very idea that there should be a robust set of overarching principles that govern relations between peoples, arguing that we should be tolerant of a plurality of approaches to promoting peace among peoples and with the environments that sustain us.

Indigenous perspectives and the Buffalo Treaty

There is an emerging scholarship on Indigenous international relations that challenges state-centric expressions of sovereignty and self-determination. As Anishinaabe scholar Hayden King (2015, 181) states, 'in our political worldviews the state and sovereignty melt away'. Indigenous nations have expressed solidarity with one another through the establishment of new confederacies, treaties and agreements that promote peace, friendship and new strategic alliances. Indigenous international relations are enduring and sacred, and making treaties with foreign countries has not prevented Indigenous nations from continuing their own diplomatic relations with one another. For example, the Treaty of Peace, Respect, and Responsibility between the Heiltsuk Nation and the Haida Nation (Crist 2014) was the first peace treaty between these two nations since the 1850s and was premised on the assumption that 'there are greater troubles facing our lands and waters and depletion of resources generated from forces outside of our nations'. The Treaty was enacted between the two Indigenous nations through a potlatch ceremony and sought to challenge a common threat posed by the state-sanctioned commercial herring fishery in Heiltsuk waters.

In 2014, another historic treaty was initiated between Indigenous nations living along the medicine line (the United States-Canada border). Iiniiwa, which is the Blackfoot name for bison, have a deep, longstanding relationship with the land, people and cultural practices of prairie ecosystems. When discussing the role of the bison on their homelands, Blackfoot scholar Leroy Little Bear (2014) pointed out that

> [a]cting as a natural bio-engineer in prairie landscapes, they shaped plant communities, transported and recycled nutrients, created habitat variability that benefited grassland birds, insects and small mammals, and provided abundant food resources for grizzly bears, wolves and humans.

Unfortunately, the widespread slaughter of bison in the nineteenth century led to the deterioration of the prairie ecosystems and with this the health and wellbeing of Blackfeet people. The decimation of the bison also impacted the cultural practices of the region's Indigenous peoples, which has prompted the need for community-led action to restore the iiniiwa to Indigenous homelands.

On 23 September 2014, eight Indigenous nations (the Blackfeet Nation, Blood Tribe, Siksika Nation, Piikani Nation, the Assiniboine and Gros Ventre Tribes of Fort Belknap Indian Reservation, the Assiniboine and Sioux Tribes of Fort Peck Indian Reservation, the Salish and Kootenai Tribes of the Confederated Salish and Kootenai Indian Reservation, and the Tsuu T'ina Nation) gathered in Blackfeet territory near Browning, Montana to sign the historic Buffalo Treaty. It involved Indigenous nations on both sides of the medicine line and called for the return of iiniiwa to the prairie ecosystems. Given that it was the first cross-border Indigenous treaty signed in over 150 years, the Buffalo

Treaty was also a way of renewing and regenerating old alliances. It outlined several community-led goals, including engaging tribes and First Nations in continuing dialogue on iiniiwa conservation; uniting the political power of the tribes and First Nations of the Northern Great Plains; advancing an international call for the restoration of the iiniiwa; engaging youth in the treaty process and strengthening and renewing ancient cultural and spiritual relationships with iiniiwa and grasslands in the Northern Great Plains.

As an example of Indigenous international relations, the above-mentioned treaty provisions demonstrate the sacred nature of treaty-making as a way for Indigenous nations 'to extend their relationships of connection to all of the different peoples of the world' (Williams 1997, 50). In addition to having Indigenous nations as signatories, the Buffalo Treaty also outlines a vision for the involvement of federal, state and provincial governments, as well as farmers, ranchers and conservation groups in the restoration of iiniiwa to Indigenous homelands. As individual Indigenous nations, these communities would have a limited ability to promote iiniiwa restoration. However, with a unified vision, they collectively exerted their self-determining authority to facilitate the return of iiniiwa to some 6.3 million acres of their homelands.

The Buffalo Treaty is also a living document that requires periodic renewal and re-interpretation. Two years after the Treaty was signed, the number of signatories had gone from eight to 21. In September 2016, signatories held a pipe ceremony in Banff National Park to honour the planned reintroduction of sixteen iiniiwa to the area. In addition to restoring the buffalo population, signatories called on the Government of Alberta in Canada to change the name of Tunnel Mountain in Banff to Sacred Buffalo Guardian Mountain. The vision for the regeneration and perpetuation of iiniiwa also entails changing the landscape to reflect the places where the iiniiwa live. New forms of Indigenous treaty-making reflect the complex diplomacies and spiritual re-awakenings that constitute Indigenous inter-national relations.

Conclusion

A power imbalance, and differences in worldviews, between states and Indigenous nations remains in our international system. Developments and critiques within the discipline of IR, and how it is theorised, highlight the struggle of Indigenous peoples to maintain their place-based existence so that their lands, cultures, communities and relationships will flourish for generations to come. Indigenous understandings of international relations come in many forms, whether through reinvigorating treaties with the natural world, (re)establishing alliances between Indigenous peoples or Indigenous advocacy in diplomatic activities within global forums. These efforts challenge the dominant state-centric system to include their different ways of understanding and structuring relations not just between peoples, but with the natural world and the planet. More specifically, they challenge the Westphalian notion of ultimate state sovereignty and seek ways of restoring self-determining authority regarding their relationships to their homelands and nations.

19

A Contemporary Perspective on Realism

FELIX RÖSCH & RICHARD NED LEBOW

Since the end of the Cold War realism has returned to its roots. Realist scholars show renewed interest in their foundational thinkers, their tragic understanding of life and politics, their practical concern for ethics and their understanding of theory as the starting point for explanatory narratives or forward-looking forecasts that are highly context dependent. Despite their different perspectives on world politics, the writings of Thucydides, Niccolò Machiavelli, Edward Hallett Carr, Reinhold Niebuhr, Arnold Wolfers, John Herz, Hans Morgenthau and Hannah Arendt demonstrate a remarkable unity of thought as they were driven by similar concerns about 'perennial problems' (Morgenthau 1962, 19). One of these problems is the depoliticisation of societies. Realists were concerned that, in modern societies, people could no longer freely express their interests in public, losing the ability to collectively contribute to their societies. Consequently, realism can be perceived as a critique of and 'corrective' (Cozette 2008, 12) to this development. It may seem strange at first, but one way to see how realism relates to today's world is to look back to its roots – via its earlier scholars – rather than dwell on some of the later developments in realist theory, such as neorealism. For this reason, this chapter will revisit realism to offer a contemporary perspective on what is, most probably, the oldest theory of IR and, most certainly, IR's most significant theory family.

The basics of a contemporary perspective on realism

Mid-twentieth century realists, often called 'classical' realists, were a diverse group of scholars. Although their geographical centre was in the United States (with some exceptions), many of them were émigrés from Europe who had been forced to leave due to the rise of fascism and communism in the

1930s. Although they shared a common humanistic worldview in the sense that they had received similar extensive secondary schooling in liberal arts and believed that people can only experience themselves as human beings by engaging with others in the public sphere, their diversity is also evidenced in their wide range of professions. Given that IR was only gradually institutionalised in Europe when the first chair was set up in light of the horrors of the First World War at the university in Aberystwyth in 1919, none of them were trained as an IR scholar. Instead, they were historians, sociologists, philosophers, lawyers and even theologians. Only retrospectively were many of them linked to IR. Even Morgenthau, arguably the best-known realist, held a professorship for political science and history, not for International Relations. Despite this diversity, however, mid-twentieth century realists agreed on a tragic vision of life – a view they shared with many of their predecessors (Lebow 2003; Williams 2005). This is because people, and more so leaders, have to make decisions on the basis of incomplete information, deal with unpredictability of their actions and cope with irreconcilable value conflicts within and among societies. Above all, they recognise that leaders must sometimes resort to unethical means (such as violence) to achieve laudable ends – and without prior knowledge that these means will accomplish the ends they seek.

This tragic outlook is understandable if we consider the contexts in which these classical realists wrote. Thucydides lived during the times of the Peloponnesian War in which Athens lost its pre-eminence in the ancient Greek world. Machiavelli's life was also influenced by repetitive conflicts in which papal, French, Spanish and other forces aimed to seize control over Northern Italy during the Renaissance Wars (1494–1559). Modern realists finally experienced with the rise of ideologies the climax of a development that had started almost two hundred years earlier. Since the Age of Enlightenment culminating in the French Revolution, people were freed from religious straightjackets. But simultaneously they had lost a sense of community that ideologies such as nationalism, liberalism or Marxism could only superficially restore – and often only at the cost of violent conflicts. Realists shared public sentiments that losing this sense of community caused a decline of commonly accepted values as exemplified in the German debate on a cultural crisis during the early decades of the twentieth century. This made them more susceptible to the temptations of ideologies. This is because ideologies provide what Arendt (1961, 469) called 'world explanations', enabling people to channel their human drives into them.

John Herz (1951) argued that the drive for self-preservation, which ensures that people care about their survival in the world by seeking food and shelter, provokes a security dilemma because people can never be certain to avoid attacks from others. Morgenthau (1930), by contrast, was more concerned about the drive to prove oneself, achieved by making contributions to one's social-political life worlds. Success is difficult because people have incomplete knowledge about themselves and their life-worlds. Any political decision must always be temporary and subject to revision if circumstances change or knowledge is being advanced. In realising that their ambitions are in vain, another tragic aspect of life comes to the fore. For Morgenthau, accepting this tragic aspect is a first step toward transcending it; people can reflect critically about their existence and come to understand that only through their own efforts can life become meaningful. In modernity, however, having lost values as a basis to make informed judgements, peoples' lives are characterised by what Steven Toulmin (1990, 35) called a 'quest for certainty', but very few manage to deal with the hardships self-critical contemplation entails. Most, as Nietzsche noted, content themselves with the illusions of being embedded in some form of community. Therefore, on the level of nation-states tragedy looms large because people live in political communities that are characterised by the same deficiencies that hamper the human condition.

Given that these drives affect people on every level, realists do not distinguish between domestic and international politics. Rather, they focus on political communities however they may be conceived because it is through peoples' relations that these human drives start to affect politics. In these relations, power plays a decisive role. Due to the drive to prove oneself, a balance of power evolves in interpersonal, intergroup and international relations to counter ambitions of political actors to gain the ability to dominate others. This balance of power is not stable but evolving because actors face a security dilemma, meaning that, due to uncertainty, actors live in constant fear. This compels them to amass further power, only causing the same reaction in their potential adversaries. Hence, it is less physical or material constraints that lead to a balance of power and more emotional insecurity. Ironically, therefore, balance of power works best when needed least because if people and communities share some form of common identity, they can cooperate more easily and do not require a balance of power.

However, human drives have an even more dramatic effect on societies beyond the evolvement of a balance of power, as they can depoliticise them. This concern is central to the realist thought of Hans J. Morgenthau. He opposed the more common friend enemy/distinction and defined the political as a universal force that is inherent in every human and that necessarily focuses on others, while at the same time it only comes into being in interpersonal relationships. The resulting discussions, in which people express their interests, create an 'arena of contestation' (Galston 2010, 391). Realising their individual capabilities and experiencing power through acting together, people develop their identities, as they gain knowledge about themselves and their life-worlds.

The tragedy of human imperfection, however, endangers the political, as it fosters the development of ideologies. Given that most people cannot face their imperfections, ideologies offer some form of ontological security. This means that ideologies provide people with a sense of order and it helps them to conceal the initial meaninglessness of life, as ideologies offer explanations to historical and current socio-political events. Particularly fascism and communism occupied the minds of classical realists, as they were the most violent ideologies during their lifetime, but they were also critical of the hubris of American liberalism and nationalism in general.

For realists, ideologies aim to retain the socio-political status quo and any human activity is geared towards sustaining this reification. The current socio-political reality is perceived as given and it cannot be fundamentally altered. The development of the political as a realm in which people can voice their interests freely and share their thoughts about the composition and purpose of their political community endangers the socio-political status quo, as it potentially encourages socio-political change. To cope with this depoliticis-ation, realists put forward what can be called an 'ethics of responsibility', to use Max Weber's term. Although realists were convinced that most people would be unwilling or incapable of taking responsibility for their lives, they still argued for an ethics in which decision-making is guided by 'intellectual honesty' (Sigwart 2013, 429). Thoughts and beliefs have to be contextualised in a self-critical process that demonstrates empathy towards the position of others. The resulting 'discourse ethic', as Arendt called it, can only happen in collectivity. American town hall meetings provided the perfect setting for Arendt to illustrate this, as they allow all people who share a common interest to congregate. As a consequence, however, people have to be prepared to change their positions and be willing to take responsibility for the moral dilemmas of (inter)national politics.

Contrary to common assumptions, realists are not apologists of the nation-state, but critical of it, aiming to avoid its dangers and transcend its shortcomings by investigating the potential of a world-state (Scheuerman 2011). For a variety of reasons, classical realists considered states to be 'blind and potent monster[s]' (Morgenthau 1962, 61). They are blind because globalisation and technological advancements not only hinder them from fulfilling their role of providing security, but endanger life on earth altogether. Particularly strong versions of this critique can be found in Aron, Herz and Morgenthau. The latter provided a disenchanted view on the prospects of humanity in one of his last public appearances, arguing that we are living in a 'dream world' because nation-states can no longer uphold the claim to have a monopoly of power over a given territory due to the development of nuclear weapons. Furthermore, the squandering of natural resources threatens the environment, leading to a 'society of waste' (Morgenthau 1972, 23). However, nation-states are also potent because in gaining sovereignty over a specific territory and a specific group of people, they exert violence on these people and on others. Nation-states universalise their own standards and even try to impose them onto others, as evidenced in the rise of fascism during the early twentieth century in Europe. After seizing power in countries like Italy, Germany, Spain and Croatia, fascist movements not only waged wars internationally (ultimately leading to the Second World War) but also exerted violence domestically by ostracising ethical, religious and socio-political minorities. Furthermore, technological advancements complicate human life-worlds, accelerating socio-political decision-making processes. This benefited the development of scientific elites, who are unaccountable to the public, but who in their attempt to socially plan the world affect people in their everyday lives greatly.

Classical realist perspectives on the European migration crisis

Since 2011, millions of people have become displaced from Syria due to the civil war there. This has been exacerbated by migration flows coming from other states in Africa and the Middle East due to various political and economic circumstances. By 2015 the issue had been declared a crisis in Europe – the destination for many of the migrants. Focusing on this crisis might not seem to be an obvious choice, but many realists were refugees or migrants themselves. Indeed, Herz (1984, 9) characterised himself as a 'traveller between all worlds' and Morgenthau was even a 'double exile' (Frankfurter 1937) after his expulsion from Germany and later Spain before arriving in the United States in 1937. Beyond this point, realism provides useful insights into this crisis as we can investigate the conditions for a peaceful coexistence of differences. This is important, as the refugee issue has been identified as one of the reasons why the British public voted to leave the European Union (EU) in the 2016 'Brexit' referendum. It has also been implicated in the rise of right-wing parties throughout Europe and the victory of Donald Trump in the 2016 US presidential election. Refugees and migrants are clearly being pictured in security discourses as a threat – and to measurable effects.

Relating the work of mid-twentieth century 'classical' realists to this modern development enables IR scholarship to understand that security is established in a discursive context, making it dependent on spatio-temporal conditions. This means security has different meanings in different contexts and therefore it is transformative (Behr 2013, 169). This puts realist thought into affinity with the critical theories that ostensibly seem opposed to it. Given that both groupings found stimulation in the same sources, one of which was Karl Mannheim's *Ideology and Utopia* (1929), this is unsurprising. One of the key concepts in Mannheim's book is the conditionality of knowledge. This means that knowledge is always bound to the socio-political environment in which it operates, stressing that universal knowledge is impossible. Applying this notion to the current refugee crisis, we understand that perceiving refugees as a threat to security is the result of human will and political agency. For example, the refugee crisis was one of the dominant drivers of British Brexit-discourses, although the UK received fewer than 40,000 asylum seekers in 2015. By comparison, approximately 890,000 refugees chose Germany as their destination the same year, making Germany the European country that accepts most refugees in relation to the overall population.

This is not to say that this process always takes place consciously as we can never be entirely sure how our writings or actions are perceived by others, but classical realism can help us to understand that humans are not only the objects of security but also its subjects. In public discourses, people have the opportunity to redefine the substance of security, instead of leaving it to international foreign policy elites. These discourses can evolve violently, as they include the interests of all involved people. To avoid this looming danger, realists stress the possibility of dialogical learning, as current scholarship calls it, to increase the potential to morph these discourses into a common good. This form of learning is based on continuous possibilities of exchange between refugees, migrants and local people and it requires all groups to demonstrate open-mindedness and empathy as well as the willingness to challenge one's own positions. As a result, security can be redefined and what is perceived to be a crisis can be eventually understood as an opportunity to create something 'which did not exist before, which was not given, not even as an object of cognition or imagination' (Arendt 1961, 151).

Recall that classical realists were sceptical of the promises of modern nation-states and argued for the establishing of a world community, eventually leading to a world state. Such a global community would help to transcend the depolitisation in modern societies and even support 'defenders of the global state to stay sober' (Scheuerman 2011, 150). Such sobriety would be beneficial to add to the academic and political debate on migration. After all, the root of the migration crisis in Europe was that certain states, and certain influential groups within them, decided to enforce the metaphorical and physical walls of their borders and limit (or block) migrants from entering due to perceiving them as a security threat to their nation. By enabling people to get together on different levels, political spheres can extrapolate beyond national borders, allowing people to exchange their interests globally and gradually develop an identity that goes beyond that of the state. It also allows for different images of the migrant, or the refugee, to gain traction – to replace the negative ones that became widespread in Europe by 2015.

The flexibility found within the classical realist literature allows people to accommodate diverse human interests. The resulting self-reflexivity and open-mindedness helps life trajectories influenced by different historical, cultural, socio-political or religious factors to be accepted. In political spheres, people are acknowledged for their differences and, through discussion, a common ground is established that is at least acceptable to citizens at a basic level. If this can be done within each state, then it is possible that it can be done at the global level. If such an end can be attained then there will be no migration crises in the future as a global citizenry will exist. Classical realists did not arrive at this conclusion straight away. Rather, scholars like Morgenthau and Niebuhr were sceptical at first of international organisations like the United Nations and the early forms of the European Union. However, they soon realised that they provide the space (if used as they had hoped) for the political to gradually evolve, as different actors can get together peacefully and exchange their ideas at the international level.

Conclusion

In this chapter we have introduced a perspective on realism that is probably unlike what may be found in other IR theory textbooks. It was our ambition to introduce students to a more nuanced perspective on realism, to set it apart from neorealism, and to demonstrate that realism can help us to develop a more critical awareness of international politics. Realism, especially in its classical form, is therefore far from being ready for the dustbin of the history of IR theory – as some critics suggest. It can serve as a stepping stone to question some of the common assumptions held in the discipline, propose solutions to some of the contemporary problems in international relations and show us how we can create more inclusive societies.

20

The 'Isms' Are Evil. All Hail the 'Isms'!

ALEX PRICHARD

In this concluding chapter I want to explore some of the problems that come with classifying IR theory in the way we do. I want to open up a problem. Why is it we call theories of world politics theories and not ideologies? To answer this question I will engage in a bit of metatheory – that is, theory about theory – to expose some of the complexities and problems that emerge once we think a little more deeply about how the 'isms' can and ought to be used. The point of this chapter is to help you to think theoretically about how the previous chapters in this book hang together. In other words, while you might have already spotted shared characteristics of the various 'isms', in this chapter I want to give you the tools to understand why those commonalities exist at all.

In short, the argument is that IR theories should be understood not only as theories but also as ideologies. The proximity and difference between theories and ideologies will become clearer as we progress, but the key point I want to make is that when we understand the ideological element in IR theory, we are better able to think critically about the enterprise of dividing IR up as a set of isms in the first place.

The chapter starts with a quick overview of the rise and fall of the isms in political studies and IR theory. Funnily enough, for many people we live in a post-ideological age, and the fact IR theorists talk about theories and not ideologies is manifest evidence of that. I then discuss some reasons we should reject the isms as a way of compartmentalising philosophical thinking in IR, and show how concept analysis and ideology critique are good alternatives. But I close by arguing that we need ideologies and our isms not only to help frame explanations of world politics but also as raw material for exposing the political and moral assumptions scholars work with. Hopefully, this final chapter should encourage you to be both playful and experimental with IR theory.

An 'ism' is a suffix that denotes a more or less systematic set of beliefs, opinions, and/or values about the world. The suffix is added when something moves from being quite specific to encompassing more expansive or general views, beliefs and attitudes. For example, Philippines president Rodrigo Duterte may have general views that are unique to him, but until he or anyone else systematises them into a coherent worldview, we are unlikely to start talking about Duterteism in the same way we would of Marxism for example.

The isms become even more expansive when more than one person contributes to or develops the initial set of views. Contemporary Marxism incorporates a vast array of ideas and theories, approaches, epistemologies and ontologies. Indeed, other isms add a large measure of Marxism to their own too, mainly to distinguish them from other sub-types. For example, there can be both orthodox or heterodox Marxism or liberal feminism and Marxist feminism, and so forth. In short, in political science the isms generally denote ideologies and their refinements.

In IR, however, we think of the isms as theories, not ideologies, which is odd. Why do we call Marxism a theory in IR, but an ideology in political science? This is not just a semantic issue. In fact it goes to the core of what IR thought of itself in the period in which it emerged as a stand-alone social science at the turn of the twentieth century. The reason IR scholars spoke of theory rather than ideology at this time was that it was generally held that international relations were not amenable to the totalising visions of the good life that we find elaborated in the architecture of the main ideologies (Wight 1966). Realists prided themselves on their ability to cut through the moral haze of world politics to the perennial problems of world politics. Realism was not an ideology, but increasingly came to be seen as a simple set of universal truths about politics.

This tendency to distinguish IR theory from ideologies was cemented at the end of the Cold War when almost everyone else also became post-ideological. This had a number of core features. The end of the Cold War galvanised a widespread consensus that liberalism was no longer an ideology, but was instead given in the structures of history, which, according to Francis Fukuyama (1989), were now coming to fruition signifying an 'end of history'. The Soviet Union, the counter-hegemonic power that offered the only existing alternative to Western liberalism, had fallen. For many, such as Fukuyama, this meant that we were entering a post-ideological age, an age in which the dominance of liberalism and the demise of its main challengers – fascism and communism – meant there simply were no other ideologies around, making liberalism the truth revealed at the end of history. Part of this account of liberalism, however, involved a very particular conception of human rationality, one in which maximising your self-interest was said to be both rational and a universal feature of the human psyche.

Institutionalism, methodological individualism and rationalism are all theoretical concepts. These are concepts that just 'do a job', words that have little invested in them politically, at least on the face of it. Those who deploy such words usually pride themselves on their non-ideological approach to theory development, proposing that concepts like these are scientific tools instead. These tools cut through the fluff of ideology to see what really motivates people. By these 'rationalist' accounts, it was not communism but self-interest that motivated the Soviets. Furthermore, it was not a global genuflection before this or that ideology that would bring order to the world, as the conflict between the Communists and Capitalists suggested, but the rather more mundane claim that 'institutions matter' (Keohane and Martin 1995) in helping interests align (Jahn 2009).

One might think that the left would have persisted in its critique of the covering up of the ideological content of liberal science, but oddly enough, large parts of the left also adopted their own variation of post-ideological thinking, around the same time. Poststructuralist theory took off at the end of the Cold War. One of the most significant criticisms of ideologies developed by poststructuralists cast them as visions of the world and history that were more significant as modes of power than descriptively accurate statements about the world and its history. Liberalism, and neoliberalism, were re-described as modes of (self-)governance rather than explanations of how the world worked. Once we accept assumptions about rationality we become the self-interested person the theory was only supposed to describe. Ideologies produce political subjects. In this way, ideologies came to be seen as inherently regulative and dominating; they were not descriptions of the world, but ways of making us act in it.

By the late 1990s these contesting philosophical and world historical changes had broken ashore in International Relations. Here, ideologies were re-described as 'theories', the details of which you can access in the preceding pages of this book. Few if any of the contributors speak of their various theories as ideological. To do so would be to invite all sorts of criticism. To recap only the criticisms above, ideologies are seen to be unscientific, dominating, moralising. In a word: *finished*. Theories, by contrast, are scientific, somewhat testable, at least nominally depoliticised, and lack the world historical and totalising visions of the good life we usually associate with ideologies. But, in IR, each ism has developed a cottage industry of its own, with its own specialist journals and degree programmes. In spite of this (perhaps because of it, who knows), almost no one debates between the theories any more. The great debates that were central to the discipline in the past seem to have faded, though there is increasing evidence that they were never really debates, let alone great (Wilson 1998)! Ironically, the isms we are dealing with in this book have never been more entrenched in the field, but nor have they been so little used as weapons by their various protagonists. We have, according to one recent view, come to 'the end of IR theory' (Dunne, Hansen and Wight 2013).

If we are not talking about ideologies in IR theory, what are we talking about? For David Lake (2011), we are talking about academic sects that have developed around each of the isms. These sects demand advanced students (usually those embarking on PhD studies) put themselves into a box, adopt an ism for life and then continue to specialise in the rituals and codas of these 'theologies'. Eventually, the ability of advanced scholars to think beyond or across and between the isms simply falls away. In our attempt to update each ism to meet the demands of the latest 'real world' event, the isms become all the more narrowly defined, or stretched to become so broadly defined as to make them practically ideologies. Either way, they become unhooked from the historical, social and geopolitical context in which they emerged. We then start repeating phrases like 'institutions matter' without understanding how they mattered during the Cold War and might matter in different ways today. This is known as 'reification'.

However, Lake understood theory in a way that made a categorical distinction between ideologies, theologies, philosophising and theory. For Lake, the isms are far broader categories of thought than theories. Theories posit the relationship between variables and generate testable hypotheses, while traditions are messier, unsystematic confluences of ideas that people need to straighten out in order to pull out those hypotheses.

For example, both liberalism and realism come from wider, more long-standing ideological traditions, but to make them theories of IR some core principles had to be identified. In this case, both traditions share the view that anarchy and material interests are key features of world politics, but they add additional variables to generate different theories. In pursuing this general pattern of 1) elaborating general assumption, 2) positing the relations of theoretical concepts, 3) generating testable hypotheses, there is no question that what counts as theory, what counts as evidence and what counts as viable IR subject matter narrows exponentially. Lake assumes that IR theories aspire to be scientific in a very narrow sense of that word (Lake 2011, 470), and then he says that those that don't are not really appropriate for IR. Meta-theoretical questions (again, theory about theory) – such as whether history has an end point or whether history is shaped by material forces or by ideas – are unscientific questions that are without final answers. Rather, we should focus on what he calls 'mid-level theory' – that is, hypotheses that can be tested against the empirical evidence: questions like, which institutions best limit violence? This is how Lake thinks we will come to understand how the world actually works, not through speculative philosophy.

This request for IR theory to ask what appear to be simpler questions is somewhat problematic. Lake's solution asks us to ignore the deeply ideological nature of the concepts we use routinely in IR's theories. Because we can no longer ask speculative questions about the coherence of back-ground assumptions and concepts, like what is capitalism, for example, we end up treating the already existing stock of IR theory as the extent of the material we might need from which to draw testable hypotheses. The fact that there is little consensus on what the state is, let alone whether it is the best institution to constrain violence, is hugely significant.

Paradoxically then, Lake's criticisms make IR theories, particularly the more esoteric ones, sound very much like ideologies, but the point is that all theories are ideologies. What he is unwilling to countenance is that his preferred approach is itself deeply infused with a standard notion of science that is also itself ideological: positiv*ism* (another ism). By this account, true knowledge is knowledge that is empirically verifiable, and only what we can experience counts as true evidence. But we could not know this about Lake unless we had a broad understanding of scientific ideologies too, like positivism and empiricism, such that we would be tooled to expose his underlying assumptions (Jackson 2011). Nothing is gained by exercising the sleight of hand so common in contemporary Anglo-American IR of declaiming everything but science to be ideological.

Before proposing a way out of this problem, let us quickly survey some of the problems that emerge when students do not think clearly about what isms are and what we are using the isms for. One might assume from the above that IR is better off without its isms and in some respects that is probably right. There is nothing to be gained for students or researchers by thinking that the isms are self-contained hypothesis generators. Nor should we welcome theories that purport to be able to explain everything, offering remedies to fix the world as general conclusions. I think anyone would be rightly suspicious of this. But there is a real problem with thinking about isms in this way in the first place – and we don't have to.

What if we change what we think ideologies are? Would this help us rethink the isms in IR too?

Ideologies are wondrous, porous, complex and evolving things that give us a unique insight into the structure of collective thought. Two well-known approaches to ideologies should open up what I mean here.

For the first approach, let's consider ideologies as a network of concepts, with the core concepts acting as nodes to which peripheral ones attach and disconnect as they evolve over time (Freeden 1996). So, for example, while liberty might be central to liberalism, peripheral concepts like white supremacy or democracy have receded and advanced in importance over time (respectively). Likewise, we should probably understand that concepts are used in particular historical contexts, which means they might have different meanings to the way we use them now (Berenskoetter 2016). Concepts like the state are themselves generative of isms, while particular meanings of a given concept can only be understood in terms of that ism.

For example, could we really understand what liberalism is without an understanding of what contemporary liberals mean by liberty? And which comes first, the ideology or the concept? This is not a frivolous argument, because unless we can adequately grasp the historical specificity of the language we use, we will be tempted to simply assume this is how our language has always been used, leaving us 'bewitched' by the present (Skinner 1998).

Once we start to interrogate key concepts, their logic, coherence and their relation to other concepts, we can map the relations of ideologies to one another. For example, both realism and liberalism share core concepts like anarchy, the state, material power and so on. But the relative importance of each can only really be understood once we see how 'peripheral' and other 'core' concepts are deployed in relation to one another, like cooperation or capitalism, institutions or hegemony. Have you ever wondered why you agree with some aspects of an ideology but not with others and agonised about how you can make sense of your split loyalty? This way of understanding the structure of ideologies better shows us the interconnected tapestry of ideologies, something we need to get used to – a worthwhile endeavour for students of IR to do with all the theories presented in this book.

So, ideologies then, like theories, are tapestries of concepts. But, let's take another step back and engage in some ideology critique to explore the second approach. What made it possible to dream up a theory like realism or liberalism in the first place? With the exception of postcolonialism and feminism, most IR theories were, broadly speaking, developed in the West by white men, predominantly from the top 1–2% of income earners, or the upper middle class. In fact, it took the emergence of feminist and postcolonial theorists to point this out. To do this, these theorists had to develop complex accounts of the world and how it hung together that took on the core concepts and assumptions of the mainstream. Contrary to Lake, it was only because feminists and postcolonial theorists (amongst others) probed the existential concepts and categories that theoretical development was possible at all. And, this involved exposing IR theories as ideological. This is how dialectical thought operates. It explores the conditions of possibility of a given way of thinking, whether that is conceptual coherence, historical specificity or whatever, and then pushes beyond it.

It is not important whether IR theories are true or not. What matters is whether they help shape our thinking such that they can guide action, scholarly, political or theological. It is because they guide action, shape it, constrain it and make sense of it that ideologies and theories should be continually scrutinised. Ideologies are the background cognitive, moral structures that shape societies and reflect their differences, and so understanding how they operate will tell us a huge amount about the world we live in.

Let's try something: turn on your television. Is there not a striking sameness to the stuff that is broadcast in most countries – especially Western ones? It's not just that there are a lot of programmes on cooking and real estate, but that the underlying assumptions behind the programmes have a certain resonance. You don't find presenters of real estate shows lamenting the unjust structures of capitalism or proclaiming that property is theft! Rather, there is a shared sense of the inevitability of the logic of property ownership or that the objective is to secure the highest price possible. Think about the way boys and girls are differently appealed to in the cartoons they watch, with gendered roles almost routinely given rather than questioned.

As Steve Smith (2007, 8) has argued, 'the option of non-theoretical accounts of the world is simply not available'. As such, you need to familiarise yourself with what theory is, how it works and how it shapes the way you see the world. Ideology critique explores the ways in which communication in general is constrained and circumscribed by taken-for-granted ideas, concepts, attitudes and theories, or the way normal language is theory bound and theory dependent. Theories, then, IR theories too, are themselves reflections of ideology. They should be subjected to critique in the same way.

Conclusion

Think of the isms and a broad understanding of them in three ways:

First, isms are ideologies and IR theories are ideologically saturated too. This is not a bad thing per se. Once we know this we should be able to both interrogate the internal coherence of the ideology and compare its virtues with others.

Second, ideologies themselves shape the society we live in. So, we ought to be able to understand our society and world politics better by exploring the ways in which ideologies shape and structure the ways in which people live and act. In many respects, then, IR theory reflects these ways of living and acting too. Thus, we can think of IR theory as itself an ideological reflection of the world around us. R. B. J. Walker (1993, 6) has made the contentious suggestion that 'theories of international relations are more interesting as aspects of contemporary world politics that need to be explained than as explanations of world politics.' You might not want to go that far, but there is no doubt that there is nothing politically or ideologically neutral about IR theory – and locating IR theories in their historical and intellectual context exposes this irreversibly.

Third, ideologies can be wrong, their values reprehensible or odious, their core assumptions preposterous. This is because they are used by people whose practices and politics we might disagree with. For Robert Cox (1981, 128), theory is not only always 'for someone and for some purpose', but it also inevitably reflects class biases. We need to be aware of this and subject theory to a range of critiques. Understanding Marxism would be the indispensable precondition of this. Doing this would be impossible if we were to deny theory-as-ideologies exist, or if we overlook how deeply implicated in ideological structures our modern way of living and thinking are.

Nothing is gained by rejecting the isms unless we at first understand the complexity of what it is we are rejecting. The isms may be evil, but we must pay due homage to them in order to develop the critical reflection we need to move beyond them.

References

Acharya, Amitav. (2014). 'Global IR and Regional Worlds: Beyond Sahibs and Munshis – A New Agenda for International Studies', Presidential Address to the 55th Annual Convention of the International Studies Association, Toronto, 26–29 March.

Acharya, Amitav. (2016). '"Idea-shift": How Ideas From the Rest are Reshaping Global Order', *Third World Quarterly* 37 (7): 1156–1170.

Acharya, Amitav and Barry Buzan. (2010). 'Why is There No Non-Western International Relations Theory? An Introduction', in *Non-Western International Relations Theory Perspectives on and beyond Asia,* edited by Amitav Acharya and Barry Buzan, 1–25. Oxon and New York: Routledge.

Agnew, John. (1994). "The Territorial Trap: The Geographical Assumptions of International Relations Theory', *Review of International Relations* 1(1): 53–80.

Archibugi, Daniele. (2004). 'Cosmopolitan Guidelines for Humanitarian Intervention'. *Alternatives 29 (1)*: 1–22.

Arendt, Hannah. (1961). *Between Past and Future: Six Exercises in Political Thought*. London: Faber & Faber.

Ayoub, Phil and David Paternotte, eds. (2014). *LGBT Activism and the Making of Europe: A Rainbow Europe?* Palgrave: New York.

Bairoch, Paul. (1993). *Economics and World History: Myths and Paradoxes*. New York: Harvester Wheatsheaf.

Behera, Navnita Chadha. (2010). 'Re-Imagining IR in India', in *Non-Western International Relations Theory Perspectives on and beyond Asia,* edited by Amitav Acharya and Barry Buzan, 92–116. Oxon and New York: Routledge.

Behr, Hartmut. (2013) 'Security Politics and Public Discourse: A Morgenthauian Approach', in *Interpreting Global Security,* edited by M. Bevir, O. Daddow, and I. Hall, London: Routledge.

Beitz, Charles. (1975). 'Justice and International Relations', *Philosophy and Public Affairs* 4 (4): 360–389.

Berenskoetter, Felix, ed. (2016). *Concepts in World Politics*. London: Sage.

Biermann, Frank. (2001). 'The Emerging Debate on the Need for a World Environment Organization: A Commentary', *Global Environmental Politics* 1 (1): 45–55.

Bigo, Didier, Philippe Bonditti and Christian Olsson. (2010). 'Mapping the European Field of Security Professionals', in *Europe's 21st Century Challenge: Delivering Liberty*, edited by Didier Bigo, Sergio Carrera, Elspeth Guild and R. B. J. Walker, 49–64. London: Routledge.

Biswas, Shampa (2014). *Nuclear Desire: Power and the Postcolonial Nuclear Order*. Minneapolis/London: University of Minnesota Press.

Blake, Michael. (2001). 'Distributive Justice, State Coercion, and Autonomy', *Philosophy and Public Affairs* 30 (3): 257–296.

Booth, Kenneth. (1991). 'Security and Emancipation', *Review of International Studies* 17(4): 313–326.

Booth, Kenneth. (1997). 'Security and Self: Reflections of a Fallen Realist', in *Critical Security Studies*, edited by K. Krause and J. C. Williams. London: UCL Press.

Boswell, Thomas. (2001). 'In Disbelief: A Suspension of American Innocence', *Washington Post*, 12 September: D01.

Boyd, Charles. G. (2001). 'Vulnerable to Hate', *Washington Post*, 12 September: A29.

Brock, Gillian. (2010). *Global Justice: A Cosmopolitan Account.* Oxford: Oxford University Press.

Brown, Garrett Wallace. (2012). 'Distributing Who Gets What and Why: Four Normative Approaches to Global Health', *Global Policy* 3 (3): 292–302.

Bull, Hedley. (1977). *The Anarchical Society: A Study of Order in World Politics*. London: Macmillan.

Butler, Judith. (2003). 'Violence, Mourning, Politics', *Studies in Gender and Sexuality* 4(1): 9–37.

Butler, Judith. (1990). *Gender Trouble*. New York: Routledge.

Buzan, Barry, Ole Wæver, and Jaap de Wilde. (1998). *Security: A New Framework for Analysis*. London: Lynne Rienner.

Caney, Simon. (2010). 'Climate Change, Human Rights and Moral Thresholds', in *Climate Ethics: Essential Readings,* edited by Stephen Gardiner, Simon Caney, Dale Jamieson and Henry Shue, 163–180. Oxford: Oxford University Press.

Caney, Simon. (2006). *Justice Beyond Borders.* Oxford: Oxford University Press.

Chowdhry, Geeta and Sheila Nair, eds. (2002) *Power, Postcolonialism and International Relations: Reading Race, Gender and Class*. New York: Routledge.

Chun, Chaesung. (2010). 'Why is There No Non-Western International Relations Theory? Reflections on and from Korea', in *Non-Western International Relations Theory Perspectives on and beyond Asia,* edited by Amitav Acharya and Barry Buzan, 69–91. New York: Routledge.

Coomaraswamy, Radhika. (2015). *Preventing Conflict, Transforming Justice, Securing the Peace: A Global Study on the Implementation of United Nations Security Council Resolution 1325.* New York: UN Women.

Corntassel, Jeff. (2008). 'Toward Sustainable Self-Determination: Rethinking the Contemporary Indigenous-Rights Discourse', *Alternatives* 33 (1): 105–132.

Cox, Robert W. and Jacobson, Harold. K. (1977). 'Decision Making', *International Social Science Journal* 29(1): 115–135.

Cox, Robert W. (1981). 'Social Forces, States and World Orders: Beyond International Relations Theory', *Millennium – Journal of International Studies* 10 (2): 126–155.

Cozette, Murielle. (2008) 'Reclaiming the Critical Dimension of Realism: Hans J. Morgenthau and the Ethics of Scholarship', *Review of International Studies* 34(1): 5–27.

Crist, Valine. (2014). 'A Peace of Mind: Haida Heiltsuk Affirm Historic Relationship', *Haida Laas: Newsletter of the Council of the Haida Nation*. Pp. 8–10.

Deudney, Daniel and G. John Ikenberry. (1999). 'The Nature and Sources of Liberal International Order'. *Review of International Studies* 25 (2): 179–196.

Dunne, Tim, Lene Hansen and Colin Wight. (2013). 'The End of International Relations Theory?', *European Journal of International Relations* 19(3): 405–425.

Dyer, Hugh. (2014). 'Climate Anarchy: Creative Disorder in World Politics', *International Political Sociology* 8 (2): 182–200.

Edkins, Jenny. (2006). 'The Local, the Global and the Troubling', *Critical Review of International Social and Political Philosophy* 9(4): 499–511.

Enloe, Cynthia. (1989). *Bananas, Beaches and Bases: Making Feminist Sense of International Politics*. London: Pandora.

Fanon, Frantz. (1967). *Black Skin, White Masks*. New York: Grove Press.

Fierke, Karin M. (2015). *Critical Approaches to International Security*, 2nd ed. Cambridge: Polity Press.

Finnemore, Martha. and Kathryn Sikkink. (1998). 'International Norm Dynamics and Political Change', *International Organization* 52(4): 887–917.

Foucault, Michel. (1976). *History of Sexuality 1*. New York: Penguin.

Foucault, Michel. (1984). 'The Order of Discourse', in M. Shapiro, *Language and Politics*. Oxford: Basil Blackwell.

Fraser, Nancy. (1995). 'From Redistribution to Recognition? Dilemmas of Justice in a "Post-Socialist" Age', *New Left Review* 212: 68–93.

Frankfurter, Felix. (1937) 'Letter to Nathan Greene', 9 December. Container 22, Manuscript Division, Library of Congress, Washington, DC.

Freeden, Michael. (1996). *Ideologies and Political Theory: A Conceptual Approach*. Oxford: Clarendon.

Galston, William. A. (2010) 'Realism in Political Theory', *European Journal of Political Theory* 9 (4): 385–411.

Goodin, Robert. (1992). *Green Political Theory*. Cambridge: Polity.

Gramsci, Antonio. (1998). *Selections from the Prison Notebooks*, London: Lawrence & Wishart.

Harris, Paul. (2010). *World Ethics and Climate Change: From International to Global Justice.* Edinburgh: Edinburgh University Press.

Handrahan, Lori. (2004). 'Conflict, Gender, Ethnicity and Post-Conflict Reconstruction', *Security Dialogue* 35 (4): 429–445.

Hardin, Garret. (1968). 'The Tragedy of the Commons'. *Science* 162: 1243–1248.

Harvey, David. (2001). *Spaces of Capital: Towards a Critical Geography*. Edinburgh: Edinburgh University Press.

Harvey, David. (2006). *Spaces of Global Capitalism: Towards a Theory of Uneven Geographical Development*. London and New York: Verso.

Harvey, David. (2009). *Cosmopolitanism and the Geographies of Freedom*. New York: Columbia University Press.

Hayden, Patrick. (2010). 'The Environment, Global Justice and World Environmental Citizenship' in *The Cosmopolitanism Reader*, edited by Garrett W. Brown and David Held, 351–372. Cambridge: Polity Press.

Hayward, Tim. (2007). 'Human Rights Versus Emission Rights: Climate Justice and the Equitable Distribution of Ecological Space', *Ethics and International Affairs* 21 (4): 431–450.

Herbert, Bob. (1994) 'In America; Terror in Toyland'. *New York Times*, December 1. Available at www.nytimes.com/1994/12/21/opinion/in-america-terror-in-toyland.html

Herz, John. (1951) *Political Realism and Political Idealism*. Chicago: University of Chicago Press.

Herz, John. (1984) *Vom Überleben: Wie ein Weltbild entstand*. Düsseldorf: Droste.

hooks, bell. (2000). *Feminist Theory: From Margin to Center*. Cambridge, MA: South End Press.

Huntington, Henry P. (2013). 'A Question of Scale: Local versus Pan-Arctic Impacts from Sea-Ice Change', in *Media and the Politics of Arctic Climate Change: When the Ice Breaks*, edited by Miyase Christensen, Annika E. Nilsson and Nina Wormbs, 114–127. Basingstoke: Palgrave Macmillan.

Hutchings, Kimberly. (2001). 'The Nature of Critique in Critical International Relations Theory', in *Critical Theory and World Politics*, edited by Richard Wyn Jones, 79–90. Boulder and London: Lynne Rienner.

Inoguchi, Takashi. (2007). 'Are There Any Theories of International Relations in Japan?', *International Relations of the Asia-Pacific* 7 (3): 369–390.

Jackson, Patrick Thaddeus. (2011). *The Conduct of Inquiry in International Relations: Philosophy of Science and its Implications for the Study of World Politics*. London: Routledge.

Jahn, Beate. (2009). 'Liberal Internationalism: From Ideology to Empirical Theory – and Back Again', *International Theory* 1(3): 409–438.

Kaldor, Mary. (2010). 'Humanitarian Intervention: Toward a Cosmopolitan Approach', in *The Cosmopolitanism Reader*, edited by Garrett W. Brown and David Held, 334–350. Cambridge: Polity Press.

Katzenstein, Peter. J. (1996). *The Culture of National Security: Norms and Identity in World Politics*. New York: Columbia University Press.

Keohane, Robert O. and Lisa L. Martin. (1995). 'The Promise of Institutionalist Theory', *International Security* 20(1): 39–51.

King, Hayden. (2015). 'The Problem with "Indigenous Peoples": Reconsidering International Indigenous Rights Activism', in *More Will Sing Their Way to Freedom: Indigenous Resistance and Resurgence*, edited by Elaine Coburn, 167–183. Halifax: Fernwood Publishing.

Krummel, John W. M. (2015). *Nishida Kitarō's Chiasmatic Chorology: Place of Dialectic, Dialectic of Place*. Bloomington: Indiana University Press.

Lake, David A. (2011). 'Why "isms" Are Evil: Theory, Epistemology, and Academic Sects as Impediments to Understanding and Progress', *International Studies Quarterly* 55(2): 465–480.

League of Nations. (1923). 'Petition to the League of Nations from the Six Nations of the Grand River', communications by the Government of the Netherlands, document C.500.1923.VII.

Lebow, Richard. N. (2003). *The Tragic Vision of Politics: Ethics, Interests, and Orders*. Cambridge: Cambridge University Press.

Lebow, Richard. N. (2011) 'German Jews and American Realism', *Constellations* 18(4): 545–566.

Lefebvre, Henri. (1991). *The Production of Space*, translated by Donald Nicholson Smith. Oxford: Blackwell.

Link, Arthur S. (1956). *Wilson: The New Freedom*, vol. 2. Princeton: Princeton University Press.

Little Bear, Leroy, Ervin Carlson, Angela Grier, Chief Earl Old Person and Tommy Christian (2014). 'Historic Treaty: Bring Buffalo Home, Heal the Prairie', *LiveScience*. Available at www.livescience.com/47998-tribal-treaty-to-restore-territory-american-bison.html

Lu, Peng. (2014). 'Pre-1949 Chinese IR: An Occluded History', *Australian Journal of International Affairs* 68 (2): 133–155.

Machiavelli, Nicollò. (1532). *The Prince*. The Harvard Classics, vol. XXXVI. Available at www.bartleby.com/36/1/prince.pdf

MacKenzie, Megan. (2010). 'Securitization and de-Securitization: Female Soldiers and the Reconstruction of Women in Post-Conflict Sierra Leone', in *Gender and International Security: Feminist Perspectives*, edited by Laura Sjoberg, 151–167. London: Routledge.

Mallavarapu, Siddharth. (2014). 'Siddharth Mallavarapu on International Asymmetries, Ethnocentrism, and a View on IR from India', *Theory Talks*, 9 February. Available at www.theory-talks.org/2014/02/theory-talk-63.html

Mannheim, Karl. (1929, 1985) *Ideology & Utopia: An Introduction to the Sociology of Knowledge*. San Diego: Harcourt.

Manuel, Chief George and Michael Posluns. (1974). *The Fourth World: An Indian Reality*. New York: Collier Macmillan Canada.

March, James. and Johan Olsen. (1998). 'The Institutional Dynamics of International Political Orders', *International Organization* 52 (4): 943–969.

McGinnis, Michael Vincent, ed. (1999). *Bioregionalism*. London: Routledge.

McGlinchey, Stephen. (2017). *International Relations*. Bristol: E-International Relations.

Mearsheimer, John J. (2002). 'Realism, the Real World and the Academy', in *Realism and Institutionalism in International Studies*, edited by Michael Brecher and Frank P. Harvey. Ann Arbor: The University of Michigan Press.

Meena, Krishnendra. (2013). 'BRICS: An Explanation in Critical Geography', *Contexto Internacional* 35(2): 565–593.

Meiser, Jeffrey. (2015). *Power and Restraint: The Rise of the United States, 1898–1941*. Washington: Georgetown University Press.

Memmi, Albert. (1991). *The Colonizer and the Colonized*. Boston: Beacon Press.

Miller, David. (2007). *National Responsibilities and Global Justice.* Oxford: Oxford University Press.

Miller, Robert J., Jacinta Ruru, Larissa Behrendt and Tracey Lindberg. (2010). *Discovering Indigenous Lands: The Doctrine of Discovery in the English Colonies*. Oxford: Oxford University Press.

Morgenthau, Hans. J. (1930) *Über die Herkunft des Politischen aus dem Wesen des Menschen*. Container 151, Manuscript Division, Library of Congress, Washington.

Morgenthau, Hans J. (1948). *Politics Among Nations: The Struggle for Power and Peace*. 7th edition. New York: McGraw-Hill.

Morgenthau, Hans. J. (1962) *Politics in the Twentieth Century*, vol. I, *The Decline of Democratic Politics*, Chicago: University of Chicago Press.

Morgenthau, Hans. J. (1972) *Science: Servant or Master?*, New York: New American Library.

Nagel, Thomas. (2005). 'The Problem of Global Justice'. *Philosophy and Public Affairs* 33 (3): 113–147.

Nash, Kate and Cath Browne. (2010). *Queer Methods and Methodologies*. New York: Ashgate.

Ollman, Bertell. (2003). *Dance of the Dialectic: Steps in Marx's Method*. University of Illinois Press.

Onuf, Nicholas G. (1989). *World of our Making. Rules and Rule in Social Theory and International Relations*. London: Routledge.

Pankhurst, Donna. (2008). 'Introduction: Gendered War and Peace', in *Gendered Peace: Women's Struggles for Post-War Justice and Reconciliation*, edited by Donna Pankhurst, 1–30. New York: Routledge.

Picq, Manuela. (2015). 'Self-Determination as Anti-Extractivism: How Indigenous Resistance Challenges World Politics', in *Restoring Indigenous Self-Determination: Theoretical and Practical Approaches*, edited by M. Woons. Bristol: E-International Relations.

Picq, Manuela and Markus Thiel. (2015). *Sexualities in World Politics: How LGBTQ Claims Shape International Relations*. Routledge: New York.

Pogge, Thomas. (1989). *Realizing Rawls*. Cornell: Cornell University Press.

Pogge, Thomas. (2001). 'Eradicating Systemic Poverty: Brief for a Global Resources Dividend', *Journal of Human Development* 2(1): 59–77.

Pogge, Thomas. (2010). 'Cosmopolitanism and Sovereignty', in *The Cosmopolitanism Reader*, edited by Garrett W. Brown and David Held, 334–350. Cambridge: Polity Press.

Puchala, Donald. J. (1997). 'Some Non-Western Perspectives on International Relations', *Journal of Peace Research* 34 (2): 129–134.

Qin, Yaqing. (2016). 'A Relational Theory of World Politics', *International Studies Review* 18 (1): 33–47.

Rawls, John. (1971). *A Theory of Justice*. Oxford: Oxford University Press.

Rich, Adrienne. (2002). *Arts of the Possible: Essays and Conversations*, London and New York: W.W. Norton & Co.

Risse, Mathias. (2008). 'Who Should Shoulder the Burden? Global Climate Change and Common Ownership of the Earth', Faculty Research Working Papers Series, John F. Kennedy School of Government, Harvard University.

Said, Edward W. (1978). *Orientalism*. New York: Random House.

Said, Edward W. (1997). *Covering Islam: How the Media and the Experts Determine How We See the Rest of the World*. New York: Vintage Books.

Sarkar, Benoy Kumar. (1919). 'Hindu Theory of International Relations', *American Political Science Review* 13 (3): 400–414.

Sedgwick, Eve Kosofsky. (1990). *Epistemology of the Closet*. Los Angeles: University of California Press.

Shue, Henry. (2014). *Climate Justice: Vulnerability and Protection*. Oxford: Oxford University Press.

Sigwart, Hans-Jörg (2013) 'The Logic of Legitimacy: Ethics in Political Realism', *Review of Politics* 75(3): 407–432.

Skinner, Quentin. (1998). *Liberty before Liberalism*. Cambridge: Cambridge University Press.

Smith, Steve. (2007). 'Introduction: Diversity and Disciplinarity', in *International Relations Theories: Discipline and Diversity*, edited by Tim Dunne, Milja Kurki and Steve Smith. Oxford: Oxford University Press.

Thucydides. (1972). *History of the Peloponnesian War*. Baltimore: Penguin Books.

Tickner, Ann J. (2016). 'Knowledge Is Power: Challenging IR's Eurocentric Narrative', *Presidential Special Issue International Studies Review* 18 (1): 157–159.

Toulmin, Stephen (1990) *Cosmopolis. The Hidden Agenda of Modernity*. Chicago: University of Chicago Press.

Toynbee, Polly. (2001). 'The Rule of Reason over Madness Died Along with the Victims', *The Guardian*, 12 September. Available at: https://www.theguardian.com/politics/2001/sep/12/september11.britainand9113

True, Jacqui. (2012). *The Political Economy of Violence against Women*. Oxford: Oxford University Press.

United Nations General Assembly. (2007). United Nations Declaration on the Rights of Indigenous Peoples resolution, adopted by the General Assembly, 2 October 2007. UN. Doc. A/ RES/61/295.

United Nations Permanent Forum on Indigenous Issues. (2006). *Who are Indigenous Peoples?* Available at www.un.org/esa/socdev/unpfii/documents/5session_factsheet1.pdf

Vivekanandan, Jayashree. (2014). 'Strategy, Legitimacy and the Imperium: Framing the Mughal Strategic Discourse', in *India's Grand Strategy: History, Theory, Cases*, edited by Kanti Bajpai, Saira Basit and V. Krishnappa, 63–85. New Delhi and Oxon: Routledge.

Walker, Rob B. J. (1993). *Inside/Outside: International Relations as Political Theory*. Cambridge: Cambridge University Press.

Wallerstein, Immanuel. (1974). *The Modern World-System I: Capitalist Agriculture and the Origins of the European World-Economy in the Sixteenth Century*. New York: Academic Press.

Waltz, Kenneth N. (1979). *Theory of International Politics*. Reading, MA: Addison-Wesley.

Wæver, Ole. (2000). 'The EU as a Security Actor: Reflections from a Pessimistic Constructivist on Postsovereign Security Orders', in *International Relations Theory and the Politics of European Integration*, edited by Morten Kelstrup and Michael C. Williams, 250–294. London: Routledge.

Wæver, Ole. (2015). 'The Theory Act: Responsibility and Exactitude as Seen from Securitization', *International Relations* 29(1): 121–127.

Wang, Yiwei and Xueqing Han. (2016). 'Why is There No Chinese IR Theory? A Cultural Perspective', in *Constructing a Chinese School of International Relations: Ongoing Debates and Sociological Realities*, edited by Yongjin Zhang and Teng-chi Chang, 52–67. Oxon and New York: Routledge.

Weber, Cynthia. (2014). 'Why is there no queer international theory?', *European Journal of International Relations* 21(1): 27–51.

Weber, Cynthia. (2016). *Queer International Relations*. New York: Oxford University Press.

Wendt, Alexander. (1992) 'Anarchy is What States Make of It: The Social Construction of Power Politics', *International Organization* 46(2): 391–425.

Wendt, Alexander. (1995) 'Constructing International Politics', *International Security* 20(1): 71–81.

White Face, Charmaine. (2013). *Indigenous Nations' Rights in the Balance: An Analysis of the Declaration on the Rights of Indigenous Peoples*. St. Paul, Minnesota: Living Justice Press.

White paper by the State Council Information Office of the People's Republic of China. (2017). 'China's Policies on Asia-Pacific Security Cooperation'. Available at http://english.gov.cn/archive/white_paper/2017/01/11/ content_281475539078636.htm

Williams, Robert A., Jr. (1997). *Linking Arms Together: American Indian Treaty Visions of Law & Peace 1600–1800*. New York: Oxford University Press.

Young, Iris Marion. (2011). *Justice and the Politics of Difference.* Princeton: Princeton University Press.

Yeophantong, Pichamon. (2013). 'Governing the World: China's Evolving Conceptions of Responsibility', *Chinese Journal of International Politics* 6 (4): 329–364.

Zellen, Barry Scott. (2009). *On Thin Ice: The Inuit, the State and the Challenge of Arctic Sovereignty.* Lanham Maryland: Lexington Books.

Note on Indexing

E-IR's publications do not feature indexes due to the prohibitive costs of assembling them. If you are reading this book in paperback and want to find a particular word or phrase you can do so by downloading a free PDF version of this book from the E-IR website.

View the e-book in any standard PDF reader such as Adobe Acrobat Reader (pc) or Preview (mac) and enter your search terms in the search box. You can then navigate through the search results and find what you are looking for. In practice, this method can prove much more targeted and effective than consulting an index.

If you are using apps (or devices) such as iBooks or Kindle to read our e-books, you should also find word search functionality in those.

You can find all of our e-books at: http://www.e-ir.info/publications

CPSIA information can be obtained
at www.ICGtesting.com
Printed in the USA
LVHW081942061220
673493LV00015B/1755

9 781910 814192